2-11 (17)
18 (20)   SEP 1 0 1999

A MIDSUMMER NIGHT'S DREAM

A MIDSUMMER NIGHT'S DREAM

William Shakespeare

Series Editor: Jane Bachman

Consulting Editor: Skip Nicholson

NTC Publishing Group
a division of NTC/CONTEMPORARY PUBLISHING COMPANY
Lincolnwood, Illinois USA

Interior illustrations: Diane Novario

Cover illustration: From the Art Collection of the Folger Shakespeare Library

Published by NTC Publishing Group, a division of NTC/Contemporary Publishing Company.
©1994 by NTC/Contemporary Publishing Company, 4255 West Touhy Avenue,
Lincolnwood (Chicago), Illinois 60646-1975 U.S.A.
Manufactured in the United States of America.
Library of Congress Catalog Card Number: 92-60874

7 8 9 0 VP 9 8 7 6 5 4

CONTENTS

Introducing Shakespeare

Most of what we know about William Shakespeare's life is based only on public records or on allusions to his work in various letters and diaries of his day. He was baptized on April 26, 1564, in Trinity Church in Stratford-upon-Avon and buried there on April 25, 1616. His birthday is usually celebrated on April 23, also the date of his death.

Stratford is in Warwickshire, a county northwest of London. In Shakespeare's time it was a small market town. His father, John Shakespeare, was a prosperous townsman who made gloves and was also a tanner as well as a dealer in farm produce. John Shakespeare held various town offices. However, in 1586 he was forced into bankruptcy because he could not pay his debts. Mary Arden, Shakespeare's mother, was the daughter of Robert Arden, a well-to-do farmer who left her money and a small estate in addition to several properties he had given her before his death. For most of their life together, the parents of William Shakespeare were reasonably well off.

William Shakespeare was the third of eight children, two of whom died before his birth and one of whom died when William was a boy. Only a sister, Joan, survived him; one of his brothers, Edmund, may have been an actor.

Shakespeare probably attended the grammar school in Stratford, where he might have learned Latin and Greek. Records show that he married Anne Hathaway, eight years his senior, in Stratford in 1582. He and Anne had three children: Susanna, born in 1583, and twins Judith and Hamnet, born in 1585. Hamnet died at the age of eleven.

The next record of Shakespeare is in 1592, when he was evidently in London. In the pamphlet *A Groatsworth of Wit*, addressed to fellow playwrights who were university graduates (as Shakespeare was not), Robert Greene bitterly refers to Shakespeare as "an upstart crow, beautified with our feathers, that with his Tyger's hart wrapt in a Player's hyde supposes he is as well able to bombast out a blanke verse as the best of you; and being an absolute *Johannes fac totum*, is in his owne conceit the only Shake-scene in a country." The phrase "Tyger's hart" refers to a line in *Henry VI, Part 3* by Shakespeare, a play probably first produced in 1591. *Johannes fac totum* means "jack-of-all-trades." Some scholars think that Shakespeare began his career as an actor, probably sometime before 1592, and that when he began to write plays, he angered many established playwrights, such as Greene.

Although the date of Shakespeare's arrival in London is not certain, it is known that some of his early plays were produced by an acting company known as Lord Pembroke's Men. He might have acted with this company as well. In 1594 he became a member of a company called Lord

Chamberlain's Men, for which he wrote many successful plays, and in 1599 he became a partner in the newly constructed Globe Theatre. This partnership assured his financial success and enabled him to invest in considerable property, both in Stratford and in London.

Shakespeare early achieved recognition as a poet, and in 1598 one writer referred to him as "mellifluous and honey-tongued" when writing of Shakespeare's long poem *Venus and Adonis*, first published in 1593. All in all, some 37 plays and 154 sonnets are attributed to Shakespeare.

Critics sometimes divide his dramatic career into four periods: the Early Period (1564–1594); the Period of Comedies and Histories (1595–1601); the Period of Tragedies (1602–1608); and the Period of Romances (1609–1616). The first attempt at publishing a collection of his plays was in 1623, when the First Folio was published. (The printer's term *folio* refers to the folding of the printed sheets.) The First Folio contains thirty-six plays. A later play, *Pericles*, was added to the second edition of the Third Folio in 1664. During his life, however, eighteen of Shakespeare's plays were published in quarto editions. (Again a printer's term, a *quarto* was a smaller, squarer book than a folio.)

In 1611 or 1612 Shakespeare returned permanently to Stratford where he wrote his last plays. The cause of Shakespeare's death at age fifty-two is unknown. His wife and both daughters survived him and are mentioned in his will, which also mentions small bequests to various friends and to the poor of Stratford.

Introducing *A Midsummer Night's Dream*

A Midsummer Night's Dream is about love, magic, and the nature of reality and illusion. Often labeled a romantic comedy, it is set in two worlds with four groups of characters. One world is the court of Theseus, Duke of Athens, and his bride-to-be, Hippolyta. The other world is the forest, inhabited by Titania and Oberon, Queen and King of the Fairies, and Puck (also known as Robin Goodfellow), a fairy whose chief delight is playing tricks. In addition, there are four lovers and a group of artisans or rustics, who rehearse and perform a play about two lovers, Pyramus and Thisbe. The plot of *A Midsummer Night's Dream* is formed by the interaction of these four groups: Theseus and Hippolyta, the fairies, the lovers, and the artisans.

There is no record of the first performance of *A Midsummer Night's Dream*. Scholars have inferred that it may have been written for the wedding of some aristocratic couple, and several such weddings in the 1590s have been suggested as suitable. The date of composition is usually thought to be around 1595. There is some evidence in Act II, Scene 1 that points to a celebration for Queen Elizabeth I at Elvetham in 1591, and other lines may refer to events in 1594. The play was first printed in 1600, and the title page states that it "hath beene sundry times publickely acted" by the Lord Chamberlain's Men. Most critics think it is the eleventh or twelfth play Shakespeare wrote and the fifth comedy.

Shakespeare used many sources for his play. Among them are Geoffrey Chaucer's "The Knight's Tale," a main source for the story of Theseus and Hippolyta; Chaucer's "The Merchant's Tale," for the idea of a king and queen of fairies intervening in human affairs; English folklore for Puck or Robin Goodfellow; and Ovid's *Metamorphoses*, probably the source for the legend of Pyramus and Thisbe.

Metamorphoses is a collection of mythological tales in verse written about A.D. 7–8. In the myth about Pyramus and Thisbe, the two are in love but forbidden by their parents to meet. Instead they communicate through a hole in the wall between their two dwellings. Deciding to elope, they agree to meet in a wood. Thisbe arrives first, is frightened by a lion, and runs off to hide, dropping her cloak as she does so. The lion, who has a bloody mouth from freshly killed prey, chews on her cloak and stains it with blood. Pyramus arrives, finds the cloak, thinks Thisbe is dead, and stabs himself. Thisbe returns, finds the lifeless Pyramus, and kills herself with his sword. This is the basis for the play-within-a-play in *A Midsummer Night's Dream*. By including the performance of the Pyramus and Thisbe play, Shakespeare is in part satirizing earlier plays, written and staged in the middle and later 1500s. Many of them, also based on myth, were poorly written, overly moralistic in tone, and badly acted. Most of Shakespeare's audiences would have recognized the plays satirized. The rehearsal and performance of the Pyramus and Thisbe play also helps to link the four groups of characters, some of whom also experience disappointment in love, though not in so permanent a way.

In *A Midsummer Night's Dream*, Shakespeare explores the difference between what we think we know through our senses and what we apprehend through imagination. How real are the worlds created in the play? What is the nature of the mortals' strange experiences? As with most plays, perhaps the best way to experience *A Midsummer Night's Dream* is to forget for awhile the world we live in and give ourselves up to the worlds Shakespeare created.

A Note on Shakespeare's Language

IMAGERY

Readers and theatregoers are immediately struck by the imagery in *A Midsummer Night's Dream*. The fairy world of Titania, Oberon, and Puck comes to life in our imagination as well as on the stage with the entrance of the first fairy, who must seek dewdrops and "hang a pearl" in every cowslip, and with Puck, who reports that the elves "creep into acorn cups." Titania then shifts our attention from this miniature world to a larger world where, because of her quarrel with Oberon, the seasons have been upset. The winds have sucked from the sea contagious fogs that now fall on the land and make the rivers overflow and the fields fill with mud. Grain rots. Crimson roses bloom amid frost.

Titania, we discover, has breathed the spicèd air of India and has brought back a child. Oberon has "heard a mermaid on a dolphin's back" sing so sweetly that "certain stars shot madly from their spheres." Life with these fairies is almost dizzying in its swoops and turns, and indeed it proves so for the lovers and for Bottom.

Shakespeare achieves vivid effects not only through imagination but through the tendency of his characters to list concrete details. Oberon is not content merely to tell Puck that he knows Titania sleeps among the flowers:

> I know a bank where the wild thyme blows,
> Where oxlips and the nodding violet grows;
> Quite overcanopied with luscious woodbine,
> With sweet musk roses and with eglantine.
> There sleeps Titania sometime of the night.

The fairies are not the only characters who are fond of listing, however. Egeus, "full of vexation," recreates the atmosphere with which Lysander has surrounded Hermia. Not only has Lysander given Hermia rhymes and sung at her window, he has showered her with "rings, gauds, conceits, trifles, nosegays, and sweetmeats." In Act III, Helena, through a list of details, perfectly characterizes the close friendship she and Hermia once had, and in Act IV Theseus proudly lists the qualities of his hounds in such detail that, finally, we can almost hear them bark.

Are these special effects, sometimes dazzling in their impact, the result of Shakespeare's art or of our imaginations? In the Prologue to *Henry V*, Shakespeare asks the audience to "piece out our imperfections with your thoughts" and "think, when we talk of horses, that you see them/Printing their proud hoofs i' the receiving earth." Although there are few imperfections in *A Midsummer Night's Dream*, it is only with our willing participation that the imagery can work its magic.

METER AND VERSE FORMS

The meter or rhythm of the language and the forms of verse in *A Midsummer Night's Dream* vary widely. Much of the play is written in blank verse, that is, unrhymed iambic pentameter—lines of five feet, with each foot containing an unstressed syllable followed by a stressed syllable. Blank verse is somewhat formal because of the length of the line; therefore, Theseus usually speaks in blank verse as befits a duke:

> What say you, Hermia? Be advised, fair maid.
>
> To you your father should be as a god, . . .

But Theseus also speaks in prose when he is conversing with the players in Act V.

Egeus too speaks in blank verse, but it is hurried—in keeping with his distress:

> Full of vexation come I, with complaint
> Against my child, my daughter Hermia.
> Stand forth, Demetrius. My noble lord,
> This man hath my consent to marry her.

The lovers sometimes speak in blank verse, sometimes in rhymed couplets, as Hermia does when promising to meet Lysander:

> By all the vows that ever men have broke,
> In number more than ever women spoke,
> In that same place thou hast appointed me
> Tomorrow truly will I meet with thee.

Puck speaks in rhymed lines of iambic pentameter:

> I jest to Oberon, and make him smile
> When I a fat and bean-fed horse beguile, . . .

He also speaks in shorter rhymed lines (trochaic tetrameter):

> Through the forest have I gone,
> But Athenian found I none
> On whose eyes I might approve
> This flower's force in stirring love.

Notice that each foot is accented on the first syllable and that the rhythm seems to bounce, suitable perhaps for a trickster.

The fairies too speak in rhymed lines of four feet:

> I do wander everywhere,
> Swifter than the moon's sphere;
> And I serve the Fairy Queen,
> To dew her orbs upon the green.

Titania and Oberon speak in trochaic tetrameter too, but they also speak in iambic pentameter with rhymed couplets:

> Out of this wood do not desire to go.
> Thou shalt remain here, whether thou wilt or no.

Although the artisans speak in prose, their play is written partly in pentameter couplets, partly in other rhyming variations.

In some ways, then, the four groups of characters are defined by the way they speak, a dramatic device that also helps provide connections between the worlds of the play.

Introducing the Globe Theatre

The Globe is the sixteenth-century theatre most closely associated with Shakespeare, for he had a financial interest in it, acted there, and wrote many of his plays for the actors at the Globe.

James Burbage built the first theatre in London, known simply as the Theatre, in 1576. In 1599 the Theatre was dismantled by Burbage's two sons, Richard and Cuthbert, and rebuilt as the Globe on the opposite side of the Thames River. Richard and Cuthbert Burbage held a half interest in the Globe, and five actors divided the other half interest, among them Shakespeare.

The Globe burned in 1613 when, during a performance of Shakespeare's *Henry VIII*, a cannon discharged backstage and touched off a fire in the thatched roof. The Globe was rebuilt on the same site, and we know something about its features from the surviving specifications for another theatre.

In 1600 Philip Henslowe built the Fortune theatre, and the contractor was directed to build the Fortune like the Globe, with at least one exception: it was to be square instead of polygonal.

There are a few other clues about the appearance of the Globe. Several period drawings and engravings of London and of theatres, including the Globe, still exist. Perhaps the most interesting recent event was the 1989 discovery and excavation of the remains of the Rose Theatre, built in London in 1586 quite near the Globe.

Suppose for a moment that you are a playgoer. It is early afternoon and you have reached the Globe on foot, or you have been rowed in a ferry across the Thames from the north side. As you approach the theatre, you see a flag flying from the top to indicate that a performance will be given today. Since the theatre holds 2,000 to 3,000 people, and most Londoners are avid playgoers, you soon find yourself in the midst of a huge throng.

When you enter the theatre, you can look up at the sky, for the circular area, or pit, in front of the stage is not roofed. Turning, you note that there are three levels of spectator's galleries on three sides of the theatre and a gallery above and at the back of the stage as well.

The floor of the theatre is about 5 ½ feet below the stage and about 70 feet in diameter. If you have only a penny to spend, this is where you will stand, elbow to elbow with other spectators, to see the performance. If you can afford more, you will ascend the stairs to one of the galleries, where you will be able to sit protected from the weather.

The stage itself is a little over forty feet wide and about twenty-seven feet deep. You have heard that the floor of the stage contains a trap door, a convenient opening for the emergence of special effects such as smoke.

At the back of the stage are two (possibly three) doors, which open inward and may be covered by curtains. The actors will appear through these doors from the tiring house, or dressing rooms, behind the stage. The central area behind the curtains may be used as a small "discovery space" for some plays. In a performance of *Hamlet*, for example, Polonius hides behind the curtain before he is stabbed.

If the gallery above and at the back of the stage is needed for the performance, there will be no spectators there. In *Romeo and Juliet*, this area represents Juliet's window, where she stands to speak to Romeo below.

The roof above the stage is decorated and is supported by at least two pillars. Above the roof is an area that probably contains ropes and pulleys for lowering and raising actors and props.

The stage itself has few props and no scenery. There may be a throne for a king, a curtained bed for Juliet, a few stools and tables for interior scenes, and candles or torches to indicate night. Exterior scenes are indicated by the actors' speeches, as in *A Midsummer Night's Dream* when Quince says, "Here's a marvelous place for our rehearsal. This green plot shall be our stage, this hawthorn brake our tiring-house." There are costumes, however, which are the property of the acting company and are not to be worn by the actors when they are not performing.

Such simple equipment enables the acting companies to pack up and tour the countryside when, on occasion, the London theatres are closed because of an outbreak of the plague.

For the moment, however, the day is warm and sunny, and the Globe is filled with an enthusiastic and noisy crowd. Your fellow "groundlings" you notice, reek somewhat of garlic, may not have had a bath recently, and tend to jostle you as they try to find a good viewing spot. But the noise lessens and you forget your surroundings as the first actor steps onto the stage.

CHARACTERS

THESEUS, *Duke of Athens*

HIPPOLYTA, *Queen of the Amazons, betrothed to Theseus*

PHILOSTRATE, *Master of the Revels*

EGEUS, *father of Hermia*

HERMIA, *daughter of Egeus, in love with Lysander*

LYSANDER, *in love with Hermia*

DEMETRIUS, *in love with Hermia and approved by Egeus*

HELENA, *in love with Demetrius*

TITANIA, *Queen of the Fairies*

OBERON, *King of the Fairies*

PUCK, *or* ROBIN GOODFELLOW

PEASEBLOSSOM
COBWEB
MOTH } *Fairies*
MUSTARDSEED

Other FAIRIES *attending Titania and Oberon*

PETER QUINCE, *a carpenter;* PROLOGUE, *in the interlude*

NICK BOTTOM, *a weaver;* PYRAMUS

FRANCIS FLUTE, *a bellows mender;* THISBE

TOM SNOUT, *a tinker;* WALL

SNUG, *a joiner;* LION

ROBIN STARVELING, *a tailor;* MOONSHINE

ATTENDANTS *on Theseus and Hippolyta*

SCENE: *Athens, and a wood near it.*

1

A MIDSUMMER NIGHT'S DREAM

ACT I

"The course of true love never did run smooth."

4   **lingers**   drags out or prolongs.

5   **stepdame or a dowager**   stepmother or a widow who has inherited property or a title from her husband.

6   **withering out**   causing to shrink. The sense of lines 4–6 is that the moon makes Theseus wait just as a stepmother or widow makes a son wait for his inheritance.

11   **solemnities**   (sə lem'ni tēz) marriage ceremonies.

16   **wooed thee with my sword**   Theseus took Hippolyta captive while fighting the Amazons, in mythology a race of female warriors.

SCENE 1

Theseus and Hippolyta are discussing their forthcoming wedding when Egeus, Hermia, Lysander, and Demetrius enter, Egeus to bring a complaint to Theseus. Hermia has been pledged to Demetrius but refuses to marry him, for she and Lysander are in love. Demetrius had once courted Helena but now loves Hermia. Theseus warns Hermia that she must obey her father. If not, she must either die or become a nun, and she must decide by the next new moon. Hermia and Lysander agree to run away, and, when Helena, who still loves Demetrius, is informed of the plan, she decides to tell Demetrius.

Athens. The palace of THESEUS.

Enter THESEUS, HIPPOLYTA, PHILOSTRATE,
and ATTENDANTS.

THESEUS.   Now, fair Hippolyta, our nuptial hour
Draws on apace; Four happy days bring in
Another moon; but, O, methinks, how slow
This old moon wanes! She lingers my desires,   4
Like to a stepdame or a dowager   5
Long withering out a young man's revenue.   6

HIPPOLYTA.   Four days will quickly steep themselves in
   night;
Four nights will quickly dream away the time;
And then the moon, like to a silver bow
New-bent in heaven, shall behold the night
Of our solemnities.   11

THESEUS.   Go, Philostrate,
Stir up the Athenian youth to merriments,
Awake the pert and nimble spirit of mirth,
Turn melancholy forth to funerals;
The pale companion is not for our pomp.
                      Exit PHILOSTRATE.
Hippolyta, I wooed thee with my sword   16
And won thy love doing thee injuries;
But I will wed thee in another key,
With pomp, with triumph and with reveling.

32   **stol'n the impression of her fantasy** dishonestly imprinted your image on her imagination.

33   **gauds, conceits** trinkets, fancy articles.

34   **knacks** knickknacks; **nosegays** bouquets.

Enter EGEUS, HERMIA, LYSANDER, *and* DEMETRIUS.

EGEUS.   Happy be Theseus, our renownèd duke!

THESEUS.   Thanks, good Egeus. What's the news with
    thee?

EGEUS.   Full of vexation come I, with complaint
    Against my child, my daughter Hermia.
    Stand forth, Demetrius. My noble lord,
    This man hath my consent to marry her.
    Stand forth, Lysander. And, my gracious duke,
    This man hath bewitched the bosom of my child.
    Thou, thou, Lysander, thou hast given her rhymes
    And interchanged love tokens with my child.
    Thou hast by moonlight at her window sung,
    With feigning voice verses of feigning love,
    And stol'n the impression of her fantasy   32
    With bracelets of thy hair, rings, gauds, conceits,   33
    Knacks, trifles, nosegays, sweetmeats, messengers   34
    Of strong prevailment in unhardened youth.
    With cunning hast thou filched my daughter's heart,
    Turned her obedience, which is due to me,
    To stubborn harshness. And, my gracious duke,
    Be it so she will not here before your Grace
    Consent to marry with Demetrius,
    I beg the ancient privilege of Athens:
    As she is mine, I may dispose of her,
    Which shall be either to this gentleman
    Or to her death, according to our law
    Immediately provided in that case.

THESEUS.   What say you, Hermia? Be advised, fair maid.
    To you your father should be as a god,
    One that composed your beauties; yea, and one
    To whom you are but as a form in wax
    By him imprinted, and within his power
    To leave the figure or disfigure it.
    Demetrius is a worthy gentleman.

HERMIA.   So is Lysander.

54 **in this kind, . . . voice** in this respect, lacking your father's approval.

68 **blood** passions.

70 **livery** costume.

71 **aye** ever; **mewed** shut in.

80 **ere** before; **patent** privilege.

THESEUS.   In himself he is;
　　But in this kind, wanting your father's voice,   54
　　The other must be held the worthier.

HERMIA.   I would my father looked but with my eyes.

THESEUS.   Rather your eyes must with his judgment
　　look.

HERMIA.   I do entreat your Grace to pardon me.
　　I know not by what power I am made bold,
　　Nor how it may concern my modesty
　　In such a presence here to plead my thoughts;
　　But I beseech your Grace that I may know
　　The worst that may befall me in this case
　　If I refuse to wed Demetrius.

THESEUS.   Either to die the death or to abjure
　　Forever the society of men.
　　Therefore, fair Hermia, question your desires,
　　Know of your youth, examine well your blood,   68
　　Whether, if you yield not to your father's choice,
　　You can endure the livery of a nun,   70
　　For aye to be in shady cloister mewed,   71
　　To live a barren sister all your life,
　　Chanting faint hymns to the cold fruitless moon.
　　Thrice-blessèd they that master so their blood,
　　To undergo such maiden pilgrimage;
　　But earthlier happy is the rose distilled,
　　Than that which, withering on the virgin thorn,
　　Grows, lives, and dies in single blessedness.

HERMIA.   So will I grow, so live, so die, my lord,
　　Ere I will yield my virgin patent up   80
　　Unto his lordship, whose unwishèd yoke
　　My soul consents not to give sovereignty.

THESEUS.   Take time to pause, and, by the next new
　　moon—
　　The sealing day betwixt my love and me,
　　For everlasting bond of fellowship—
　　Upon that day either prepare to die
　　For disobedience to your father's will,

89   **Diana's altar**   Diana was the goddess of the moon and protector of women; **protest**   vow.

92   **crazèd**   unsound, flawed.

98   **estate unto**   settle on you, give to.

106   **avouch it to his head**   declare it to his face.

116   **schooling**   admonition.

120   **extenuate**   relax.

Or else to wed Demetrius, as he would,
Or on Diana's altar to protest   89
For aye austerity and single life.

DEMETRIUS.   Relent, sweet Hermia; and, Lysander, yield
Thy crazèd title to my certain right.   92

LYSANDER.   You have her father's love, Demetrius;
Let me have Hermia's. Do you marry him.

EGEUS.   Scornful Lysander! True, he hath my love,
And what is mine my love shall render him.
And she is mine, and all my right of her
I do estate unto Demetrius.   98

LYSANDER.   I am, my lord, as well derived as he,
As well possessed; my love is more than his;
My fortunes every way as fairly ranked,
If not with vantage, as Demetrius';
And, which is more than all these boasts can be,
I am beloved of beauteous Hermia.
Why should not I then prosecute my right?
Demetrius, I'll avouch it to his head,   106
Made love to Nedar's daughter, Helena,
And won her soul; and she, sweet lady, dotes,
Devoutly dotes, dotes in idolatry,
Upon this spotted and inconstant man.

THESEUS.   I must confess that I have heard so much,
And with Demetrius thought to have spoke thereof;
But, being overfull of self-affairs,
My mind did lose it. But, Demetrius, come,
And come, Egeus. You shall go with me;
I have some private schooling for you both.   116
For you, fair Hermia, look you arm yourself
To fit your fancies to your father's will,
Or else the law of Athens yields you up—
Which by no means we may extenuate—   120
To death or to a vow of single life.
Come, my Hippolyta. What cheer, my love?
Demetrius and Egeus, go along.
I must employ you in some business

125 **Against**   in preparation for.

126 **nearly**   closely.

s.d.* **Exeunt**   (ek'sē ənt) they leave.

130 **Belike**   very likely.

131 **Beteem**   allow.

135 **different in blood**   that is, the lovers had inherited different statuses in life.

136 **cross**   vexation; **enthralled to low**   captivated by one lower in status.

137 **misgrafted**   not well matched.

143 **momentany**   lasting but a minute.

145 **collied**   blackened.

146 **in a spleen**   on a sudden impulse.

152 **teach . . . patience**   teach us to bear our trial patiently.

155 **fancy's**   love's.

*stage directions

Against our nuptial, and confer with you 125
Of something nearly that concerns yourselves. 126

EGEUS. With duty and desire we follow you.
                    Exeunt all but LYSANDER *and* HERMIA.   n

LYSANDER.   How now, my love! Why is your cheek so
    pale?
How chance the roses there do fade so fast?

HERMIA.   Belike for want of rain, which I could well 130
Beteem them from the tempest of my eyes. 131

LYSANDER.   Ay me! For aught that I could ever read,
Could ever hear by tale or history,
The course of true love never did run smooth;
But, either it was different in blood— 135

HERMIA.   O cross! Too high to be enthralled to low. 136

LYSANDER.   Or else misgrafted in respect of years— 137

HERMIA.   O spite! Too old to be engaged to young.

LYSANDER.   Or else it stood upon the choice of
    friends—

HERMIA.   O hell, to choose love by another's eyes!

LYSANDER.   Or, if there were a sympathy in choice,
War, death, or sickness did lay siege to it
Making it momentany as a sound, 143
Swift as a shadow, short as any dream,
Brief as the lightning in the collied night 145
That, in a spleen, unfolds both heaven and earth, 146
And ere a man hath power to say "Behold!"
The jaws of darkness do devour it up.
So quick bright things come to confusion.

HERMIA.   If then true lovers have been ever crossed,
It stands as an edict in destiny.
Then let us teach our trial patience, 152
Because it is a customary cross,
As due to love as thoughts, and dreams, and sighs,
Wishes, and tears, poor fancy's followers. 155

167   **do observance . . . May**   celebrate May Day.

171   Note that the style has changed from blank verse to rhymed couplets.

173–174 **Carthage queen . . . false Trojan**   In mythology, Dido, Queen of Carthage, killed herself when the Trojan Aeneas left her.

183   **lodestars**   guiding stars.

186   **were favor so**   Helena wishes that a pleasing appearance or good looks (favor) were as catching as sickness.

LYSANDER.   A good persuasion. Therefore, hear me,
  Hermia.
 I have a widow aunt, a dowager
 Of great revenue, and she hath no child.
 From Athens is her house remote seven leagues;
 And she respects me as her only son.
 There, gentle Hermia, may I marry thee,
 And to that place the sharp Athenian law
 Cannot pursue us. If thou lovest me, then,
 Steal forth thy father's house tomorrow night;
 And in the wood, a league without the town,
 Where I did meet thee once with Helena
 To do observance to a morn of May,   167
 There will I stay for thee.

HERMIA.   My good Lysander!
 I swear to thee, by Cupid's strongest bow,
 By his best arrow with the golden head,
 By the simplicity of Venus' doves,   171
 By that which knitteth souls and prospers loves,
 And by that fire which burned the Carthage queen, 173
 When the false Trojan under sail was seen,
 By all the vows that ever men have broke,
 In number more than ever women spoke,
 In that same place thou hast appointed me
 Tomorrow truly will I meet with thee.

LYSANDER.   Keep promise, love. Look, here comes
  Helena.

     Enter HELENA.

HERMIA.   God speed, fair Helena! Whither away?

HELENA.   Call you me fair? That fair again unsay.
 Demetrius loves your fair. O happy fair!
 Your eyes are lodestars, and your tongue's sweet air 183
 More tuneable than lark to shepherd's ear
 When wheat is green, when hawthorn buds appear.
 Sickness is catching. O, were favor so,   186
 Yours would I catch, fair Hermia, ere I go;

190   **bated**   excepted.

191   **translated**   transformed.

209   **Phoebe**   (fē'bē) the moon.

210   **glass**   mirror.

215   **faint**   pale; **wont**   (wônt) accustomed.

219   **stranger companies**   the company of strangers.

My ear should catch your voice, my eye your eye,
My tongue should catch your tongue's sweet melody.
Were the world mine, Demetrius being bated,   190
The rest I'd give to be to you translated.   191
O, teach me how you look and with what art
You sway the motion of Demetrius' heart.

HERMIA.   I frown upon him, yet he loves me still.

HELENA.   O, that your frowns would teach my smiles
    such skill!

HERMIA.   I give him curses, yet he gives me love.

HELENA.   O, that my prayers could such affection move!

HERMIA.   The more I hate, the more he follows me.

HELENA.   The more I love, the more he hateth me.

HERMIA.   His folly, Helena, is no fault of mine.

HELENA.   None, but your beauty. Would that fault were
    mine!

HERMIA.   Take comfort. He no more shall see my face.
    Lysander and myself will fly this place.
    Before the time I did Lysander see
    Seemed Athens as a paradise to me.
    O, then, what graces in my love do dwell,
    That he hath turned a heaven unto a hell?

LYSANDER.   Helen, to you our minds we will unfold.
    Tomorrow night, when Phoebe doth behold   209
    Her silver visage in the watery glass,   210
    Decking with liquid pearl the bladed grass,
    A time that lovers' flights doth still conceal,
    Through Athens' gates have we devised to steal.

HERMIA.   And in the wood, where often you and I
    Upon faint primrose beds were wont to lie,   215
    Emptying our bosoms of their counsel sweet,
    There my Lysander and myself shall meet,
    And thence from Athens turn away our eyes
    To seek new friends and stranger companies.   219
    Farewell, sweet playfellow. Pray thou for us,

226   **How . . . be**   How happy some are in comparison with some others.

231   **admiring of**   wondering at.

232   **holding no quantity**   that is, without dimension, unsubstantial.

237   **figure**   symbolize.

242   **eyne**   eyes.

249   **dear expense**   that is, a trouble worth taking.

And good luck grant thee thy Demetrius!
Keep word, Lysander. We must starve our sight
From lovers' food till morrow deep midnight.

LYSANDER.　I will, my Hermia. (*Exit* HERMIA.) Helena,
　　adieu.
　　As you on him, Demetrius dote on you!

Exit LYSANDER.

HELENA.　How happy some o'er other some can be!　　226
　　Through Athens I am thought as fair as she.
　　But what of that? Demetrius thinks not so;
　　He will not know what all but he do know.
　　And as he errs, doting on Hermia's eyes,
　　So I, admiring of his qualities.　　231
　　Things base and vile, holding no quantity,　　232
　　Love can transpose to form and dignity.
　　Love looks not with the eyes, but with the mind,
　　And therefore is winged Cupid painted blind.
　　Nor hath Love's mind of any judgment taste;
　　Wings and no eyes figure unheedy haste.　　237
　　And therefore is Love said to be a child,
　　Because in choice he is so oft beguiled.
　　As waggish boys in game themselves forswear,
　　So the boy Love is perjured everywhere.
　　For ere Demetrius looked on Hermia's eyne,　　242
　　He hailed down oaths that he was only mine;
　　And when this hail some heat from Hermia felt,
　　So he dissolved, and showers of oaths did melt.
　　I will go tell him of fair Hermia's flight:
　　Then to the wood will he tomorrow night
　　Pursue her; and for this intelligence
　　If I have thanks, it is a dear expense.　　249
　　But herein mean I to enrich my pain,
　　To have his sight thither and back again.

Exit.

2   **generally**   Bottom means the opposite, "individually."

3   **scrip**   script.

6   **interlude**   short play, comedy.

11   **marry**   mild oath, originally "by the Virgin Mary."

SCENE 2

Six rustics or "rude mechanicals" plan to write and produce a play based on the story of Pyramus and Thisbe for the Duke at his marriage festivities. Parts are assigned by Quince, and plans are made to meet to rehearse in secret in the woods.

Athens.

Enter QUINCE *the carpenter,* SNUG *the joiner,*
BOTTOM *the weaver,* FLUTE *the bellows mender,*
SNOUT *the tinker, and* STARVELING *the tailor.*

QUINCE.   Is all our company here?

BOTTOM.   You were best to call them generally, man by   2
man, according to the scrip.   3

QUINCE.   Here is the scroll of every man's name, which
is thought fit, through all Athens, to play in our
interlude before the Duke and the Duchess, on his   6
wedding day at night.

BOTTOM.   First, good Peter Quince, say what the play
treats on, then read the names of the actors, and so
grow to a point.

QUINCE.   Marry, our play is, "The most lamentable   11
comedy, and most cruel death of Pyramus and
Thisbe."

BOTTOM.   A very good piece of work, I assure you, and
a merry. Now, good Peter Quince, call forth your
actors by the scroll. Masters, spread yourselves.

QUINCE.   Answer as I call you. Nick Bottom, the
weaver.

BOTTOM.   Ready. Name what part I am for, and
proceed.

QUINCE.   You, Nick Bottom, are set down for Pyramus.

BOTTOM.   What is Pyramus? A lover, or a tyrant?

QUINCE.   A lover, that kills himself most gallant for
love.

27   **condole** lament.

28–30   **humor** inclination; **I . . . split.** Bottom says he could play Hercules (Ercles) unusually well (rarely). *To tear a cat* means "to rant and rave," and *to make all split* means "to make a commotion." The stage tradition of a ranting Hercules comes from a Roman play by Seneca, *Hercules Furens.*

35   **Phibbus' car** Bottom's mistake for the chariot of Phoebus (fē'bəs), the sun god.

50   **small** high-pitched.

BOTTOM.   That will ask some tears in the true
      performing of it. If I do it, let the audience look to
      their eyes. I will move storms; I will condole in   27
      some measure. To the rest. Yet my chief humor is   28
      for a tyrant. I could play Ercles rarely, or a part to
      tear a cat in, to make all split.

      "The raging rocks
      And shivering shocks
      Shall break the locks
        Of prison gates;
      And Phibbus' car   35
      Shall shine from far,
      And make and mar
        The foolish Fates."

This was lofty! Now name the rest of the players.
This is Ercles' vein, a tyrant's vein. A lover is
more condoling.

QUINCE.   Francis Flute, the bellows mender.

FLUTE.   Here, Peter Quince.

QUINCE.   Flute, you must take Thisbe on you.

FLUTE.   What is Thisbe? A wandering knight?

QUINCE.   It is the lady that Pyramus must love.

FLUTE.   Nay, faith, let not me play a woman. I have a
      beard coming.

QUINCE.   That's all one. You shall play it in a mask, and
      you may speak as small as you will.   50

BOTTOM.   An I may hide my face, let me play Thisbe
      too. I'll speak in a monstrous little voice, "Thisne,
      Thisne!" "Ah Pyramus, my lover dear! Thy Thisbe
      dear, and lady dear!"

QUINCE.   No, no, you must play Pyramus and, Flute,
      you Thisbe.

BOTTOM.   Well, proceed.

QUINCE.   Robin Starveling, the tailor.

STARVELING.   Here, Peter Quince.

63   **Pyramus' father**   Neither Pyramus' father nor Thisbe's parents appear in the interlude.

80   **aggravate**   Bottom means "moderate" or "soften."

82   **an 'twere**   as if it were.

QUINCE. Robin Starveling, you must play Thisbe's mother. Tom Snout, the tinker.

SNOUT. Here, Peter Quince.

QUINCE. You, Pyramus' father; myself, Thisbe's father;   63
Snug, the joiner, you, the lion's part; and, I hope here is a play fitted.

SNUG. Have you the lion's part written? Pray you, if it be, give it me, for I am slow of study.

QUINCE. You may do it extempore, for it is nothing but roaring.

BOTTOM. Let me play the lion too. I will roar, that I will do any man's heart good to hear me. I will roar that I will make the Duke say, "Let him roar again, let him roar again."

QUINCE. An you should do it too terribly, you would fright the Duchess and the ladies, that they would shriek; and that were enough to hang us all.

ALL. That would hang us, every mother's son.

BOTTOM. I grant you, friends, if you should fright the ladies out of their wits, they would have no more discretion but to hang us; but I will aggravate my   80
voice so, that I will roar you as gently as any sucking dove; I will roar you an 'twere any   82
nightingale.

QUINCE. You can play no part but Pyramus; for Pyramus is a sweet-faced man, a proper man as one shall see in a summer's day, a most lovely, gentlemanlike man. Therefore you must needs play Pyramus.

BOTTOM. Well, I will undertake it. What beard were I best to play it in?

QUINCE. Why, what you will.

92   **discharge**   perform.

93–94   **purple-in-grain**   dyed a deep red; **French-crown color** color of a French *crown*, a gold coin.

96–97   **no hair at all**   bald from French disease (syphilis).

99   **con**   memorize.

103   **devices**   plans.

107–108   **obscenely**   Bottom may mean "seemly"; **be perfect**   that is, know your lines perfectly.

110   **hold or cut bowstrings**   an archer's expression. Bottom probably means "keep your promises, or give up the play."

BOTTOM.   I will discharge it in either your straw color   92
    beard, your orange-tawny beard, your purple-in-   93
    grain beard, or your French-crown color beard, your
    perfect yellow.

QUINCE.   Some of your French crowns have no hair at   96
    all, and then you will play barefaced. But, masters,
    here are your parts. And I am to entreat you,
    request you, and desire you, to con them by   99
    tomorrow night, and meet me in the palace wood, a
    mile without the town, by moonlight. There will we
    rehearse; for if we meet in the city, we shall be
    dogged with company, and our devices known. In   103
    the meantime I will draw a bill of properties, such
    as our play wants. I pray you, fail me not.

BOTTOM.   We will meet, and there we may rehearse
    most obscenely and courageously. Take pains, be   107
    perfect. Adieu.

QUINCE.   At the Duke's oak we meet.

BOTTOM.   Enough; hold or cut bowstrings.   110

                                        Exeunt.

A MIDSUMMER NIGHT'S DREAM

ACT II

*"What thou seest when thou dost wake,
Do it for thy true love take."*

3   **Thorough**   through.

4   **pale**   enclosure.

9   **dew her orbs**   sprinkle dew on circles (fairy rings). A circle formed in the grass and caused by fungi was once thought to be caused by fairies dancing in a ring.

10   **cowslips**   English primroses having yellow flowers; **pensioners**   retainers or body guards.

13   **savors**   sweet smells.

16   **lob**   bumpkin, yokel.

17   **anon**   soon.

20   **passing fell and wrath**   exceedingly fierce and wrathful or angry.

23   **changeling**   child exchanged for another by the fairies; here, the stolen child.

SCENE 1

Puck (Robin Goodfellow) and a fairy discuss the discord between the King and Queen of the fairies. When Titania and Oberon enter, they continue their quarrel. Oberon wants Titania to give him the child she rescued when its mother died, but she refuses. Oberon vows revenge by putting the juice of a flower, love-in-idleness, in Titania's eyes while she sleeps. When she awakes, she will fall in love with the first being she sees. While Puck goes to find the flower, Demetrius appears, pursued by a lovesick Helena. Oberon, overhearing them, tells Puck to put the juice of the flower in the Athenian youth's eyes so that he will fall in love with Helena.

A wood near Athens.
Enter a FAIRY *at one door,*
and ROBIN GOODFELLOW (PUCK) *at another.*

PUCK.   How now, spirit, whither wander you?

FAIRY.   Over hill, over dale,
    Thorough bush, thorough brier,   3
Over park, over pale,   4
    Thorough flood, thorough fire,
I do wander everywhere
Swifter than the moon's sphere;
    And I serve the Fairy Queen,
    To dew her orbs upon the green.   9
    The cowslips tall her pensioners be.   10
    In their gold coats spots you see;
    Those be rubies, fairy favors,
    In those freckles live their savors: 13
I must go seek some dewdrops here,
And hang a pearl in every cowslip's ear.
Farewell, thou lob of spirits; I'll be gone.   16
Our Queen and all her elves come here anon.   17

PUCK.   The King doth keep his revels here tonight.
Take heed the Queen come not within his sight.
For Oberon is passing fell and wrath,   20
Because that she as her attendant hath
A lovely boy, stolen from an Indian king;
She never had so sweet a changeling.   23

31

26   **perforce**   forcibly.

30   **square**   quarrel.

34   **Robin Goodfellow**   here, another name for Puck.

36   **Skim milk**   that is, steal the cream; **quern**   hand mill for grinding grain.

37   **bootless . . . churn**   makes the housewife churn in vain (bootless), meaning that Puck prevents the cream from turning to butter.

38   **bear no barm**   Puck prevents ale from fermenting and producing yeast (barm).

40–41   **Those that . . . luck**   that is, you do not annoy those who call you Hobgoblin and Puck rather than Robin Goodfellow.

50   **dewlap**   loose skin on the neck.

54   **"tailor" cries**   perhaps because tailors sit on the floor to sew, with a pun on *tail*.

55   **quire**   choir, company.

57   **wasted**   spent.

And jealous Oberon would have the child
Knight of his train, to trace the forests wild.
But she perforce withholds the lovèd boy,   26
Crowns him with flowers, and makes him all her joy.
And now they never meet in grove or green,
By fountain clear, or spangled starlight sheen,
But they do square, that all their elves for fear   30
Creep into acorn cups and hide them there.

FAIRY.   Either I mistake your shape and making quite,
Or else you are that shrewd and knavish sprite
Called Robin Goodfellow. Are not you he   34
That frights the maidens of the villagery,
Skim milk, and sometimes labor in the quern,   36
And bootless make the breathless housewife churn,   37
And sometime make the drink to bear no barm;   38
Mislead night wanderers, laughing at their harm?
Those that Hobgoblin call you, and sweet Puck,   40
You do their work, and they shall have good luck.
Are not you he?

PUCK.   Thou speakest aright;
I am that merry wanderer of the night.
I jest to Oberon, and make him smile
When I a fat and bean-fed horse beguile,
Neighing in likeness of a filly foal;
And sometimes lurk I in a gossip's bowl,
In very likeness of a roasted crab,
And when she drinks, against her lips I bob
And on her withered dewlap pour the ale.   50
The wisest aunt, telling the saddest tale,
Sometime for three-foot stool mistaketh me;
Then slip I from her bum, down topples she,
And "tailor" cries, and falls into a cough;   54
And then the whole quire hold their hips and laugh, 55
And waxen in their mirth, and neeze, and swear
A merrier hour was never wasted there.   57
But, room, fairy! Here comes Oberon.

FAIRY.   And here my mistress. Would that he were
gone!

63   **Tarry** (tar'ē) wait; **wanton** headstrong or willful creature.

66   **Corin** Corin and Phillida (line 68) are traditional names for pastoral lovers.

67   **pipes of corn** instrument made from stalks of grain.

71   **buskined** wearing buskins, tall laced boots.

75   **Glance . . . Hippolyta** make allusions to my relationship with Hippolyta.

78–80   **Perigenia** Perigouna. She and Aegles (ēg'lēs, line 79) were two of Theseus' mistresses. Ariadne (ar'ē ad'nē) in line 80 helped Theseus escape the labyrinth after killing the Minotaur. Antiopa (an tī'ō pa) is sometimes another name for Hippolyta but here may be another person.

82   **middle summer's spring** beginning of midsummer.

83   **mead** meadow.

84   **pavèd** with a pebbly bottom.

86   **ringlets** dances performed in a circle or ring.

90   **contagious** noxious or injurious.

91   **pelting** paltry or insignificant.

92   **overborne their continents** run over their banks.

Enter, from one side, OBERON, *with his train;*
from the other, TITANIA, *with hers.*

OBERON. Ill met by moonlight, proud Titania.

TITANIA. What, jealous Oberon! Fairies, skip hence.
I have forsworn his bed and company.

OBERON. Tarry, rash wanton. Am not I thy lord? 63

TITANIA. Then I must be thy lady; but I know
When thou hast stolen away from fairyland,
And in the shape of Corin sat all day, 66
Playing on pipes of corn, and versing love 67
To amorous Phillida. Why art thou here
Come from the farthest steppe of India,
But that, forsooth, the bouncing Amazon,
Your buskined mistress and your warrior love, 71
To Theseus must be wedded, and you come
To give their bed joy and prosperity.

OBERON. How canst thou thus for shame, Titania,
Glance at my credit with Hippolyta, 75
Knowing I know thy love to Theseus?
Didst thou not lead him through the glimmering night
From Perigenia, whom he ravishèd? 78
And make him with fair Ægles break his faith,
With Ariadne and Antiopa?

TITANIA. These are the forgeries of jealousy:
And never, since the middle summer's spring, 82
Met we on hill, in dale, forest, or mead, 83
By pavèd fountain or by rushy brook, 84
Or in the beachèd margent of the sea,
To dance our ringlets to the whistling wind, 86
But with thy brawls thou hast disturbed our sport.
Therefore the winds, piping to us in vain,
As in revenge, have sucked up from the sea
Contagious fogs which, falling in the land, 90
Have every pelting river made so proud, 91
That they have overborne their continents. 92
The ox hath therefore stretched his yoke in vain,
The ploughman lost his sweat, and the green corn

95   **beard**   bristlelike growth on the top of oats, wheat, or barley.

97   **murrain flock**   flock that died of the plague.

98   **nine men's morris**   a game played on a board or on a square marked out on the grass.

99   **quaint mazes**   intricate paths to be followed on foot; **wanton**   luxuriant.

101–102   **human mortals want . . . carol blessed**   The sense is that, though the weather has been like winter, the comfort of hymns and carols of that season is lacking.

109   **Hiems'**   winter's.

113   **wonted liveries**   usual garments; **mazèd**   bewildered.

115   **progeny**   offspring.

116   **debate**   quarrel.

117   **original**   origin.

121   **henchman**   attendant.

123   **vot'ress . . . order**   woman who had vowed to serve Titania.

129   **wanton**   playful.

Hath rotted ere his youth attained a beard;   95
The fold stands empty in the drownèd field,
And crows are fatted with the murrain flock;   97
The nine men's morris is filled up with mud;   98
And the quaint mazes in the wanton green,   99
For lack of tread, are undistinguishable.
The human mortals want their winter here;   101
No night is now with hymn or carol blessed.
Therefore the moon, the governess of floods,
Pale in her anger, washes all the air,
That rheumatic diseases do abound.
And thorough this distemperature we see
The seasons alter: hoary-headed frosts
Fall in the fresh lap of the crimson rose,
And on old Hiems' thin and icy crown   109
An odorous chaplet of sweet summer buds
Is, as in mockery, set. The spring, the summer,
The childing autumn, angry winter, change
Their wonted liveries, and the mazèd world   113
By their increase now knows not which is which.
And this same progeny of evil comes   115
From our debate, from our dissension;   116
We are their parents and original.   117

OBERON.   Do you amend it, then; it lies in you.
    Why should Titania cross her Oberon?
    I do but beg a little changeling boy,
    To be my henchman.

TITANIA.   Set your heart at rest.   121
    The fairy land buys not the child of me.
    His mother was a vot'ress of my order,   123
    And in the spicèd Indian air by night
    Full often hath she gossiped by my side
    And sat with me on Neptune's yellow sands,
    Marking th' embarkèd traders on the flood
    When we have laughed to see the sails conceive
    And grow big-bellied with the wanton wind;   129
    Which she, with pretty and with swimming gait
    Following— her womb then rich with my young
        squire—

37

142   **spare**   shun.

149   **Since**   when.

158   **vestal**   vestal virgin, in classical mythology, one of the
virgins who served the goddess Vesta. Here it is a
complimentary allusion to Elizabeth I, the virgin queen, as a
votaress of Diana, the virgin moon goddess. Some critics
cite this as evidence that this play was performed for
Elizabeth in 1591 at Elvetham.

161   **might**   could.

Would imitate, and sail upon the land
To fetch me trifles, and return again
As from a voyage, rich with mechandise.
But she, being mortal, of that boy did die;
And for her sake do I rear up her boy,
And for her sake I will not part with him.

OBERON.   How long within this wood intend you stay?

TITANIA.   Perchance till after Theseus' wedding day.
If you will patiently dance in our round
And see our moonlight revels, go with us;
If not, shun me, and I will spare your haunts.   142

OBERON.   Give me that boy, and I will go with thee.

TITANIA.   Not for thy fairy kingdom. Fairies, away!
We shall chide downright, if I longer stay.
                              Exeunt TITANIA *with her train.*

OBERON.   Well, go thy way. Thou shalt not from this
    grove
Till I torment thee for this injury.
My gentle Puck, come hither. Thou rememb'rest
Since once I sat upon a promontory,   149
And heard a mermaid on a dolphin's back
Uttering such dulcet and harmonious breath
That the rude sea grew civil at her song,
And certain stars shot madly from their spheres
To hear the sea-maid's music?

PUCK.   I remember.

OBERON.   That very time I saw, but thou couldst not,
Flying between the cold moon and the earth,
Cupid all armed. A certain aim he took
At a fair vestal thronèd by the west,   158
And loosed his love shaft smartly from his bow,
As it should pierce a hundred thousand hearts.
But I might see young Cupid's fiery shaft   161
Quenched in the chaste beams of the watery moon,
And the imperial vot'ress passèd on,

168   **love-in-idleness**   the wild pansy.

174   **leviathan**   sea monster.

185   **page**   that is, the changeling child.

192   **and wood**   and mad, insane.

195   **adamant**   hard, unyielding. *Adamant* was sometimes used to refer to the lodestone or magnet, which helps to explain Helena's reference to being drawn to Demetrius.

In maiden meditation, fancy-free.
Yet marked I where the bolt of Cupid fell:
It fell upon a little western flower,
Before milk-white, now purple with love's wound,
And maidens call it love-in-idleness.   168
Fetch me that flower; the herb I showed thee once.
The juice of it on sleeping eyelids laid
Will make or man or woman madly dote
Upon the next live creature that it sees.
Fetch me this herb, and be thou here again
Ere the leviathan can swim a league.   174

PUCK.   I'll put a girdle round about the earth
In forty minutes.

                          Exit.

OBERON.   Having once this juice,
I'll watch Titania when she is asleep
And drop the liquor of it in her eyes.
The next thing then she waking looks upon,
Be it on lion, bear, or wolf, or bull,
On meddling monkey, or on busy ape,
She shall pursue it with the soul of love.
And ere I take this charm from off her sight,
As I can take it with another herb,
I'll make her render up her page to me.   185
But who comes here? I am invisible,
And I will overhear their conference.

       Enter DEMETRIUS, HELENA *following him.*
DEMETRIUS.   I love thee not; therefore pursue me not.
Where is Lysander and fair Hermia?
The one I'll slay; the other slayeth me.
Thou told'st me they were stol'n unto this wood;
And here am I, and wood within this wood   192
Because I cannot meet my Hermia.
Hence, get thee gone, and follow me no more.

HELENA.   You draw me, you hardhearted adamant!   195
But yet you draw not iron, for my heart

214   **impeach**   call into question.

215   **To leave**   by leaving.

220   **Your virtue is my privilege**   Your goodness is my safeguard; **For that**   because.

227   **brakes**   thickets.

230   **The story shall be changed**   That is, in the myth, Apollo chased Daphne, who was saved by being turned into a laurel tree. Here, it is Helena who pursues Demetrius.

Is true as steel. Leave you your power to draw,
And I shall have no power to follow you.

DEMETRIUS.   Do I entice you? Do I speak you fair?
Or rather do I not in plainest truth
Tell you I do not nor I cannot love you?

HELENA.   And even for that do I love you the more.
I am your spaniel; and, Demetrius,
The more you beat me, I will fawn on you.
Use me but as your spaniel, spurn me, strike me,
Neglect me, lose me; only give me leave,
Unworthy as I am, to follow you.
What worser place can I beg in your love —
And yet a place of high respect with me —
Than to be used as you use your dog?

DEMETRIUS.   Tempt not too much the hatred of my
    spirit,
For I am sick when I do look on thee.

HELENA.   And I am sick when I look not on you.

DEMETRIUS.   You do impeach your modesty too much   214
To leave the city and commit yourself   215
Into the hands of one that loves you not,
To trust the opportunity of night
And the ill counsel of a desert place
With the rich worth of your virginity

HELENA.   Your virtue is my privilege. For that   220
It is not night when I do see your face,
Therefore I think I am not in the night;
Nor doth this wood lack worlds of company,
For you, in my respect, are all the world.
Then how can it be said I am alone
When all the world is here to look on me?

DEMETRIUS.   I'll run from thee and hide me in the
    brakes,   227
And leave thee to the mercy of wild beasts.

HELENA.   The wildest hath not such a heart as you.
Run when you will. The story shall be changed: 230

233 **bootless** fruitless.

235 **stay thy questions** wait for your talk.

240 **Your wrongs . . . sex** Your bad treatment of me forces me to act in a way that disgraces my sex.

244 **upon** by.

250 **oxlips** pale yellow wildflowers with a sweet scent.

251 **woodbine** honeysuckle, a shrub with very fragrant white, yellow, or red blooms.

252 **musk roses** white roses; **eglantine** a wild, pink rose.

253 **sometime of** for part of.

256 **Weed** garment.

Apollo flies and Daphne holds the chase,
The dove pursues the griffin, the mild hind
Makes speed to catch the tiger—bootless speed,   233
When cowardice pursues and valor flies.

DEMETRIUS.   I will not stay thy questions. Let me go!   235
Or if thou follow me, do not believe
But I shall do thee mischief in the wood.

HELENA.   Ay, in the temple, in the town, the field,
You do me mischief. Fie, Demetrius!
Your wrongs do set a scandal on my sex.   240
We cannot fight for love, as men may do;
We should be wooed, and were not made to woo.

                            Exit DEMETRIUS.

I'll follow thee and make a heaven of hell,
To die upon the hand I love so well.   244

                                    Exit.

OBERON.   Fare thee well, nymph. Ere he do leave this
     grove,
Thou shalt fly him, and he shall seek thy love.

                 Enter PUCK.
Hast thou the flower there? Welcome, wanderer.

PUCK.   Ay, there it is.

OBERON.   I pray thee, give it me.
I know a bank where the wild thyme blows,
Where oxlips and the nodding violet grows;   250
Quite overcanopied with luscious woodbine,   251
With sweet musk roses, and with eglantine.   252
There sleeps Titania sometime of the night,   253
Lulled in these flowers with dances and delight;
And there the snake throws her enameled skin,
Weed wide enough to wrap a fairy in.   256
And with the juice of this I'll streak her eyes,
And make her full of hateful fantasies.
Take thou some of it, and seek through this grove.
A sweet Athenian lady is in love
With a disdainful youth. Anoint his eyes,

3 **cankers** cankerworms.

4 **reremice** (rēr'mīs) bats.

7 **quaint** dainty.

But do it when the next thing he espies
May be the lady. Thou shalt know the man
By the Athenian garments he hath on.
Effect it with some care that he may prove
More fond on her than she upon her love;
And look thou meet me ere the first cock crow.

PUCK.   Fear not, my lord, your servant shall do so.

Exeunt.

SCENE 2

Titania bids her fairies to sing and dance, and, when she falls asleep, Oberon squeezes the juice of the flower in her eyes. Lysander and Hermia, escaping Hermia's father, enter the wood and lie down to sleep. Puck, thinking that Lysander is the Athenian youth mentioned by Oberon, puts the love juice in Lysander's eyes. When Lysander awakes and spies Helena, he immediately falls in love with her.

The wood.

Enter TITANIA, *with her train.*

TITANIA.   Come, now a roundel and a fairy song;
   Then, for the third part of a minute, hence—
   Some to kill cankers in the musk rose buds,   3
   Some war with reremice for their leathern wings   4
   To make my small elves coats, and some keep back
   The clamorous owl, that nightly hoots and wonders
   At our quaint spirits. Sing me now asleep.   7
   Then to your offices, and let me rest.

Song.

FIRST FAIRY.   You spotted snakes with double tongue,
            Thorny hedgehogs, be not seen;

47

13   **Philomel**   (fil'ə mel') the nightingale, a small bird. The male sings a melodious song at night.

36   **ounce**   lynx.

37   **Pard**   leopard.

Newts and blindworms, do no wrong,
Come not near our Fairy Queen.

CHORUS.　Philomel, with melody　　　　　　　　　　13
　　　　Sing in our lullaby;
　　Lulla, lulla, lullaby, lulla, lulla, lullaby.
　　　　Never harm
　　　　Nor spell nor charm
　　Come our lovely lady nigh.
　　So, good night, with lullaby.

FIRST FAIRY.　Weaving spiders, come not here;
　　　　Hence, you long-legged spinners,
　　　　　　hence!
　　Beetles black, approach not near;
　　　　Worm nor snail, do no offense.

CHORUS.　Philomel, with melody
　　　　Sing in our sweet lullaby;
　　Lulla, lulla, lullaby, lulla, lulla, lullaby.
　　　　Never harm
　　　　Nor spell nor charm
　　Come our lovely lady nigh.
　　So, good night, with lullaby.

(TITANIA *sleeps*.)

SECOND FAIRY.　Hence, away! Now all is well.
　　　　One aloof stand sentinel.

Exeunt FAIRIES.

Enter OBERON *and squeezes the flower on*
TITANIA's *eyelids*.
OBERON.　What thou seest when thou dost wake,
　　Do it for thy true love take;
　　Love and languish for his sake.
　　Be it ounce, or cat, or bear,　　　　　　　36
　　Pard, or boar with bristled hair,　　　　　37
　　In thy eye that shall appear
　　When thou wak'st, it is thy dear.
　　Wake when some vile thing is near.

Exit.

48   **troth**   promise of true love.

51   **take . . . innocence**   that is, take my meaning as an
        expression of my innocent intentions.

52   **Love . . . conference**   that is, lovers must interpret each
        other's words in a loving way.

60   **beshrew**   curse.

63   **human**   kindly, courteous.

Enter LYSANDER *and* HERMIA.

LYSANDER.   Fair love, you faint with wandering in the
    wood;
    And to speak truth, I have forgot our way.
We'll rest us, Hermia, if you think it good,
    And tarry for the comfort of the day.

HERMIA.   Be it so, Lysander. Find you out a bed,
    For I upon this bank will rest my head.

LYSANDER.   One turf shall serve as pillow for us both;
    One heart, one bed, two bosoms, and one troth.   48

HERMIA.   Nay, good Lysander; for my sake, my dear,
    Lie further off yet. Do not lie so near.

LYSANDER.   O, take the sense, sweet, of my innocence!   51
    Love takes the meaning in love's conference.   52
    I mean that my heart unto yours is knit,
    So that but one heart we can make of it:
    Two bosoms interchainèd with an oath —
    So then two bosoms and a single troth.
    Then by your side no bed-room me deny,
    For lying so, Hermia, I do not lie.

HERMIA.   Lysander riddles very prettily.
    Now much beshrew my manners and my pride,   60
    If Hermia meant to say Lysander lied.
    But, gentle friend, for love and courtesy
    Lie further off, in human modesty.   63
    Such separation as may well be said
    Becomes a virtuous bachelor and a maid,
    So far be distant; and, good night, sweet friend.
    Thy love ne'er alter till thy sweet life end!

LYSANDER.   Amen, amen, to that fair prayer, say I,
    And then end life when I end loyalty!
    Here is my bed. Sleep give thee all his rest!

HERMIA.   With half that wish the wisher's eyes be
    pressed!
                                    (They sleep.)

74   **approve**   test.

84   **Churl**   rustic, boor, or miser (in that he withholds his love).

85   **owe**   own.

92   **darkling**   in the dark.

95   **the lesser is my grace**   the less I am favored.

102–103   **no marvel . . . thus**   that is, no wonder Demetrius flies from me as he would from a monster.

Enter PUCK.

PUCK.   Through the forest have I gone,
But Athenian found I none
On whose eyes I might approve   74
This flower's force in stirring love.
Night and silence.—Who is here?
Weeds of Athens he doth wear.
This is he, my master said,
Despisèd the Athenian maid;
And here the maiden, sleeping sound,
On the dank and dirty ground.
Pretty soul, she durst not lie
Near this lack-love, this kill-courtesy.
Churl, upon thy eyes I throw   84
All the power this charm doth owe.   85
When thou wak'st, let love forbid
Sleep his seat on thy eyelid.
So awake when I am gone;
For I must now to Oberon.

                                                    Exit.

Enter DEMETRIUS *and* HELENA, *running.*

HELENA.   Stay, though thou kill me, sweet Demetrius.

DEMETRIUS.   I charge thee, hence, and do not haunt me
    thus.

HELENA.   O, wilt thou darkling leave me? Do not so.   92

DEMETRIUS.   Stay, on thy peril! I alone will go.

                                                    Exit.

HELENA.   O, I am out of breath in this fond chase!
The more my prayer, the lesser is my grace.   95
Happy is Hermia, wheresoe'er she lies,
For she hath blessèd and attractive eyes.
How came her eyes so bright? Not with salt tears;
If so, my eyes are oftener washed than hers.
No, no, I am as ugly as a bear,
For beasts that meet me run away for fear.
Therefore no marvel though Demetrius   102
Do, as a monster, fly my presence thus.

104   **glass**   mirror.

105   **compare**   view; **sphery eyne**   eyes like stars in their spheres.

121   **will**   desire.

What wicked and dissembling glass of mine 104
Made me compare with Hermia's sphery eyne? 105
But who is here? Lysander on the ground?
Dead, or asleep? I see no blood, no wound.
Lysander, if you live, good sir, awake.

LYSANDER. (*Awaking*) And run through fire I will for
    thy sweet sake.
  Tranparent Helena! Nature shews art,
  That through thy bosom makes me see thy heart.
  Where is Demetrius? Oh, how fit a word
  Is that vile name to perish on my sword!

HELENA. Do not say so, Lysander; say not so.
  What though he love your Hermia? Lord, what
    though?
  Yet Hermia still loves you. Then be content.

LYSANDER. Content with Hermia? No! I do repent
  The tedious minutes I with her have spent.
  Not Hermia but Helena I love.
  Who will not change a raven for a dove?
  The will of man is by his reason swayed, 121
  And reason says you are the worthier maid.
  Things growing are not ripe until their season;
  So, I being young, till now ripe not to reason.
  And touching now the point of human skill,
  Reason becomes the marshal to my will
  And leads me to your eyes, where I o'erlook
  Love's stories, written in love's richest book.

HELENA. Wherefore was I to this keen mockery born?
  When at your hands did I deserve this scorn?
  Is 't not enough, is 't not enough, young man,
  That I did never, no, nor never can,
  Deserve a sweet look from Demetrius' eye,
  But you must flout my insufficiency?
  Good troth, you do me wrong, good sooth, you do,
  In such disdainful manner me to woo.
  But fare you well. Perforce I must confess
  I thought you lord of more true gentleness.

140 **abused** treated badly.

145 **heresies** opinions at variance with accepted beliefs.

156 **cruel prey** act of preying.

160 **of all loves** for love's sake.

O, that a lady, of one man refused,
Should of another therefore be abused!   140

Exit.

LYSANDER.   She sees not Hermia. Hermia, sleep thou
    there,
  And never mayst thou come Lysander near!
  For as a surfeit of the sweetest things
  The deepest loathing to the stomach brings,
  Or as the heresies that men do leave   145
  Are hated most of those they did deceive,
  So thou, my surfeit and my heresy,
  Of all be hated, but the most of me!
  And, all my powers, address your love and might
  To honor Helen and to be her knight!

Exit.

HERMIA.   (Awaking) Help me, Lysander, help me! Do
    thy best
  To pluck this crawling serpent from my breast!
  Ay me, for pity! What a dream was here!
  Lysander, look how I do quake with fear.
  Methought a serpent ate my heart away,
  And you sat smiling at his cruel prey.   156
  Lysander! What, removed? Lysander! Lord!
  What, out of hearing? Gone? No sound, no word?
  Alack, where are you? Speak, an if you hear;
  Speak, of all loves! I swoon almost with fear.   160
  No? Then I well perceive you are not nigh.
  Either death, or you, I'll find immediately.

Exit.

A MIDSUMMER NIGHT'S DREAM

ACT III

"Lord, what fools these mortals be!"

2   **Pat**   promptly.

4   **brake**   hedge, thicket; **tiring-house**   dressing room.

7   **bully**   worthy.

12   **By 'r lakin, a parlous fear**   By our ladykin (the Virgin Mary), an alarming fear.

23   **eight and six**   alternate lines of eight and six syllables, like a ballad.

SCENE 1

The rustics meet to rehearse the play, but Puck seizes the opportunity to play a trick on Bottom by giving him an ass's head. Unaware of his transformation, Bottom is astonished to see his friends run from him in fear. Titania awakes, sees Bottom, and falls in love with him.

The wood. TITANIA *lying asleep.*

Enter QUINCE, SNUG, BOTTOM, FLUTE, SNOUT, *and* STARVELING.

BOTTOM.   Are we all met?

QUINCE.   Pat, pat; and here's a marvelous convenient   2
place for our rehearsal. This green plot shall be our
stage, this hawthorn brake our tiring-house, and we   4
will do it in action as we will do it before the duke.

BOTTOM.   Peter Quince?

QUINCE.   What sayest thou, bully Bottom?   7

BOTTOM.   There are things in this comedy of Pyramus
and Thisbe that will never please. First, Pyramus
must draw a sword to kill himself, which the ladies
cannot abide. How answer you that?

SNOUT.   By 'r lakin, a parlous fear.   12

STARVELING.   I believe we must leave the killing out,
when all is done.

BOTTOM.   Not a whit. I have a device to make all well.
Write me a prologue, and let the prologue seem to
say, we will do no harm with out swords, and that
Pyramus is not killed indeed; and for the more
better assurance, tell them that I Pyramus am not
Pyramus, but Bottom the weaver. This will put
them out of fear.

QUINCE.   Well, we will have such a prologue, and it
shall be written in eight and six.   23

BOTTOM.   No, make it two more; let it be written in
eight and eight.

38   **defect**   effect, another of Bottom's errors.

58–60   **bush of thorns and a lantern**   bundle of thornbush sticks to be used as fuel. The man in the moon was traditionally shown with such a bundle and a lantern; **disfigure**   Quince means "figure"; **present**   represent.

SNOUT.   Will not the ladies be afeard of the lion?

STARVELING.   I fear it, I promise you.

BOTTOM.   Masters, you ought to consider with
yourselves: to bring in — God shield us! — a lion
among ladies is a most dreadful thing. For there is
not a more fearful wildfowl than your lion living,
and we ought to look to 't.

SNOUT.   Therefore another prologue must tell he is not
a lion.

BOTTOM.   Nay, you must name his name, and half his
face must be seen through the lion's neck, and he
himself must speak through, saying thus, or to the
same defect — "Ladies," or, "Fair ladies, I would   38
wish you," or, "I would request you," or, "I would
entreat you, not to fear, not to tremble; my life for
yours. If you think I come hither as a lion, it were
pity of my life. No, I am no such thing; I am a man
as other men are." And there indeed let him name
his name, and tell them plainly he is Snug the
joiner.

QUINCE.   Well, it shall be so. But there is two hard
things: that is, to bring the moonlight into a
chamber; for, you know, Pyramus and Thisbe meet
by moonlight.

SNOUT.   Doth the moon shine that night we play our
play?

BOTTOM.   A calendar, a calendar! Look in the almanac.
Find out moonshine, find out moonshine. (*They
look at an almanac.*)

QUINCE.   Yes, it doth shine that night.

BOTTOM.   Why, then may you leave a casement of the
great chamber window where we play open, and the
moon may shine in at the casement.

QUINCE.   Ay; or else one must come in with a bush of   58
thorns and a lantern, and say he comes to disfigure,
or to present, the person of moonshine. Then, there

67–68 **loam** mixture of clay, water, sand, straw, and so forth
used in making bricks or walls; **roughcast** mixture of lime
and gravel used to cover exterior walls.

76 **hempen homespuns** rustics dressed in clothes woven of
coarse fabric made from the hemp plant.

is another thing: we must have a wall in the great chamber; for Pyramus and Thisbe, says the story, did talk through the chink of a wall.

SNOUT.   You can never bring in a wall. What say you, Bottom?

BOTTOM.   Some man or other must present Wall. And let him have some plaster, or some loam, or some roughcast about him, to signify wall; and let him hold his fingers thus, and through that cranny shall Pyramus and Thisbe whisper.   67

QUINCE.   If that may be, then all is well. Come, sit down, every mother's son, and rehearse your parts. Pyramus, you begin. When you have spoken your speech, enter into that brake, and so every one according to his cue.

Enter PUCK *behind.*

PUCK.   What hempen homespuns have we swaggering here,   76
So near the cradle of the Fairy Queen?
What, a play toward! I'll be an auditor;
An actor too perhaps, if I see cause.

QUINCE.   Speak, Pyramus. Thisbe, stand forth.

BOTTOM.   "Thisbe, the flowers of odious savors sweet—"

QUINCE.   Odors, odors.

BOTTOM.   "—odors savors sweet;
So hath thy breath, my dearest Thisbe dear.
But hark, a voice! Stay thou but here awhile,
and by and by I will to thee appear."

Exit.

PUCK.   A stranger Pyramus than e'er play'd here.

Exit.

FLUTE.   Must I speak now?

94   **brisky juvenal** lively youth; **eke** also; **Jew** intended only to rhyme with *hue* and echo the first syllable of *juvenal*.

97   **Ninus** the mythical founder of Nineveh. His wife, Semiramis, was supposed to have founded Babylon, where the story of Pyramus and Thisbe takes place.

103   **fair** handsome.

QUINCE.   Ay, marry must you; for you must understand
he goes but to see a noise that he heard, and is to
come again.

FLUTE.   "Most radiant Pyramus, most lily-white of hue,
Of color like the red rose on triumphant brier,
Most brisky juvenal, and eke most lovely Jew,   94
As true as truest horse, that yet would never tire,
I'll meet thee, Pyramus, at Ninny's tomb."

QUINCE.   "Ninus' tomb," man. Why, you must not   97
speak that yet. That you answer to Pyramus. You
speak all your part at once, cues and all. Pyramus
enter. Your cue is past; it is, "never tire."

FLUTE.   O—"As true as truest horse, that yet would
never tire."

          Enter PUCK, *and* BOTTOM *as* PYRAMUS,
            wearing an ass's head.

BOTTOM.   "If I were fair, Thisbe, I were only thine."   103

QUINCE.   O monstrous! O strange! We are haunted.
Pray, masters! Fly, masters! Help!
    Exeunt QUINCE, SNUG, FLUTE, SNOUT, *and* STARVELING.

PUCK.   I'll follow you, I'll lead you about a round,
Through bog, through bush, through brake, through
    brier.
Sometimes a horse I'll be, sometime a hound,
A hog, a headless bear, sometime a fire;
And neigh, and bark, and grunt, and roar, and burn,
Like horse, hound, hog, bear, fire, at every turn.
                             Exit.

BOTTOM.   Why do they run away? This is a knavery of
them to make me afeard.

               Enter SNOUT.

SNOUT.   O Bottom, thou art changed! What do I see on
thee?

BOTTOM.   What do you see? You see an ass head of
your own, do you?
                         Exit SNOUT.

119   **translated**   transformed.

125   **ouzel cock**   male blackbird.

127   **throstle**   song thrush.

132   **whose note . . . mark**   many a man pays attention because it seems to be calling "cuckold." (A cuckold is the husband of an unfaithful wife.)

134   **set his wit to**   use his mind to answer.

135–136 **Who . . . so**   Who would call the bird a liar though he cry "cuckoo" ever so much?

146   **gleek**   jest.

Enter QUINCE.

QUINCE.   Bless thee, Bottom! Bless thee! Thou art
    translated.   119

                                              Exit.

BOTTOM.   I see their knavery. This is to make an ass of
    me, to fright me, if they could. But I will not stir
    from this place, do what they can. I will walk up
    and down here, and I will sing, that they shall hear
    I am not afraid.

                                           (*Sings.*)

      The ouzel cock so black of hue,   125
         With orange-tawny bill,
      The throstle with his note so true,   127
         The wren with little quill—

TITANIA.   (*Awaking*) What angel wakes me from my
    flowery bed?

BOTTOM.   (*Sings*)
      The finch, the sparrow, and the lark,
         The plainsong cuckoo gray,
      Whose note full many a man doth mark,   132
         And dares not answer nay—
    for, indeed, who would set his wit to so foolish a   134
    bird? Who would give a bird the lie, though he cry   135
    "cuckoo" never so?

TITANIA.   I pray thee, gentle mortal, sing again.
    Mine ear is much enamoured of thy note;
    So is mine eye enthrallèd to thy shape;
    And thy fair virtue's force perforce doth move me
    On the first view to say, to swear, I love thee.

BOTTOM.   Methinks, mistress, you should have little
    reason for that. And yet, to say the truth, reason
    and love keep little company together nowadays—
    the more the pity, that some honest neighbors will
    not make them friends. Nay, I can gleek upon   146
    occasion.

TITANIA.   Thou art as wise as thou art beautiful.

150–151 **serve . . . turn**   answer my purpose.

154   **rate**   rank.

166   **gambol in his eyes**   frolic in his sight.

BOTTOM.   Not so, neither. But if I had wit enough to
    get out of this wood, I have enough to serve mine   150
    own turn.

TITANIA.   Out of this wood do not desire to go.
    Thou shalt remain here, whether thou wilt or no.
    I am a spirit of no common rate.   154
    The summer still doth tend upon my state,
    And I do love thee. Therefore, go with me.
    I'll give thee fairies to attend on thee,
    And they shall fetch thee jewels from the deep,
    And sing while thou on pressèd flowers dost sleep.
    And I will purge thy mortal grossness so
    That thou shalt like an airy spirit go.
    Peaseblossom! Cobweb! Moth! and Mustardseed!

Enter PEASEBLOSSOM, COBWEB, MOTH, *and* MUSTARDSEED.

FIRST FAIRY.   Ready.

SECOND FAIRY.   And I.

THIRD FAIRY.   And I.

FOURTH FAIRY.   And I.

ALL.   Where shall we go?

TITANIA.   Be kind and courteous to this gentleman.
    Hop in his walks, and gambol in his eyes;   166
    Feed him with apricocks and dewberries,
    With purple grapes, green figs, and mulberries;
    The honey bags steal from the humble-bees,
    And for night tapers crop their waxen thighs,
    And light them at the fiery glowworm's eyes,
    To have my love to bed and to arise;
    And pluck the wings from painted butterflies,
    To fan the moonbeams from his sleeping eyes.
    Nod to him, elves, and do him courtesies.

FIRST FAIRY.   Hail, mortal!

SECOND FAIRY.   Hail!

THIRD FAIRY.   Hail!

FOURTH FAIRY.   Hail!

184–185 **If I cut . . . you** (Cobwebs were once used to stop
bleeding.)

193–194 **your patience** what you have endured. (Mustard is eaten
with beef.)

201 **weeps** causes dew.

202 **enforcèd** violated.

BOTTOM.   I cry your worship's mercy, heartily. I beseech your worship's name.

COBWEB.   Cobweb.

BOTTOM.   I shall desire you of more acquaintance, good Master Cobweb. If I cut my finger, I shall make 184 bold with you. Your name, honest gentleman?

PEASEBLOSSOM.   Peaseblossom.

BOTTOM.   I pray you, commend me to Mistress Squash, your mother, and to Master Peascod, your father. Good Master Peaseblossom, I shall desire you of more acquaintance too. Your name, I beseech you, Sir?

MUSTARDSEED.   Mustardseed.

BOTTOM.   Good Master Mustardseed, I know your 193 patience well. That same cowardly, giantlike ox-beef hath devoured many a gentleman of your house. I promise you your kindred hath made my eyes water ere now. I desire your more acquaintance, good Master Mustardseed.

TITANIA.   Come, wait upon him; lead him to my bower. The moon methinks looks with a watery eye; And when she weeps, weeps every little flower, 201 Lamenting some enforcèd chastity. 202 Tie up my lover's tongue, bring him silently.

Exeunt.

5   **night-rule**   misrule.

17   **noll**   noddle, head.

21   **russet-pated choughs**   (chufs) reddish-brown birds of the crow family.

SCENE 2

Puck tells Oberon of Titania's love and the trick he played on Bottom. He discovers, however, that he has put the love juice in the eyes of the wrong Athenian. Hermia awakes to discover that Lysander is gone, and she accuses Demetrius of killing him. Lysander now declares his love for Helena, who accuses him, Demetrius, and Hermia of mocking her. Demetrius upbraids Lysander for being unkind in pretending to love Helena, and Hermia accuses Helena of stealing Lysander's affections. Oberon now instructs Puck to put a different herb in Lysander's eyes to undo the damage. Puck does so, but not before he urges both Demetrius and Lysander to fight by hiding and imitating the voice first of one and then the other.

The wood.

Enter OBERON.

OBERON. I wonder if Titania be awaked;
Then, what it was that next came in her eye,
Which she must dote on in extremity.

Enter PUCK.

Here comes my messenger. How now, mad spirit!
What night-rule now about this haunted grove?   5

PUCK. My mistress with a monster is in love.
Near to her close and consecrated bower,
While she was in her dull and sleeping hour,
A crew of patches, rude mechanicals,
That work for bread upon Athenian stalls,
Were met together to rehearse a play
Intended for great Theseus' nuptial day.
The shallowest thickskin of that barren sort,
Who Pyramus presented, in their sport
Forsook his scene and entered in a brake.
When I did him at this advantage take,
An ass's noll I fixèd on his head.   17
Anon his Thisbe must be answered,
And forth my mimic comes. When they him spy,
As wild geese that the creeping fowler eye,
Or russet-pated choughs, many in sort,   21
Rising and cawing at the gun's report,

30   **yielders**   those who yield to fear.

36   **latched**   captured.

53   **whole**   intact.

55   **brother's**   the sun's; **th' Antipodes**   (an tip'ə dēz') people
on the opposite side of the earth.

Sever themselves and madly sweep the sky,
So, at his sight, away his fellows fly;
And, at our stamp, here o'er and o'er one falls;
He murder cries, and help from Athens calls.
Their sense thus weak, lost with their fears thus
    strong,
Made senseless things begin to do them wrong,
For briers and thorns at their apparel snatch;
Some sleeves, some hats, from yielders all things
    catch.   30
I led them on in this distracted fear,
And left sweet Pyramus translated there,
When in that moment, so it came to pass,
Titania waked, and straightway loved an ass.

OBERON.   This falls out better than I could devise.
  But hast thou yet latched the Athenian's eyes   36
  With the love juice, as I did bid thee do?

PUCK.   I took him sleeping—that is finished too—
  And the Athenian woman by his side,
  That, when he waked, of force she must be eyed.

         Enter HERMIA *and* DEMETRIUS.
OBERON.   Stand close. This is the same Athenian.

PUCK.   This is the woman, but not this the man.

DEMETRIUS.   O, why rebuke you him that loves you so?
  Lay breath so bitter on your bitter foe.

HERMIA.   Now I but chide; but I should use thee worse,
  For thou, I fear, hast given me cause to curse.
  If thou hast slain Lysander in his sleep,
  Being o'er shoes in blood, plunge in the deep,
  And kill me too.
  The sun was not so true unto the day
  As he to me. Would he have stolen away
  From sleeping Hermia? I'll believe as soon
  This whole earth may be bored, and that the moon   53
  May through the center creep, and so displease
  Her brother's noontide with th' Antipodes.   55

72   **doubler tongue**   more forked; more deceitful.

85–87   **For debt . . . stay**   Demetrius is overcome by weariness and sorrow, a debt that he will be able in a small way to pay back if he stays awhile; sleep will offer (tender) some relief from the sorrow.

It cannot be but thou hast murdered him;
So should a murderer look, so dead, so grim.

DEMETRIUS.   So should the murdered look, and so
    should I,
Pierced through the heart with your stern cruelty.
Yet you, the murderer, look as bright, as clear
As yonder Venus in her glimmering sphere.

HERMIA.   What's this to my Lysander? Where is he?
Ah, good Demetrius, wilt thou give him me?

DEMETRIUS.   I had rather give his carcass to my hounds.

HERMIA.   Out, dog! Out, cur! Thou driv'st me past the
    bounds
Of maiden's patience. Hast thou slain him, then?
Henceforth be never numbered among men.
O, once tell true, tell true, even for my sake.
Durst thou have looked upon him being awake?
And hast thou killed him sleeping? O brave touch!
Could not a worm, an adder, do so much?
An adder did it; for with doubler tongue   72
Than thine, thou serpent, never adder stung.

DEMETRIUS.   You spend your passion on a misprised
    mood.
I am not guilty of Lysander's blood,
Nor is he dead, for aught that I can tell.

HERMIA.   I pray thee, tell me then that he is well.

DEMETRIUS.   An if I could, what should I get therefor?

HERMIA.   A privilege never to see me more.
And from thy hated presence part I so.
See me no more, whether he be dead or no.

                                                    Exit.

DEMETRIUS.   There is no following her in this fierce
    vein.
Here therefore for a while I will remain.
So sorrow's heaviness doth heavier grow
For debt that bankrupt sleep doth sorrow owe,   85
Which now in some slight measure it will pay,

90   **misprision**   mistake; **ensue**   follow.

92   **that, one man holding troth**   in that, one man keeping
        true faith in love.

93   **confounding oath on oath**   breaking promise after
        promise.

96   **fancy-sick**   lovesick.

104   **apple**   pupil.

113   **fee**   reward.

If for his tender here I make some stay.

(Lies down and sleeps.)

OBERON.   What hast thou done? Thou hast mistaken quite,
And laid the love juice on some true love's sight.
Of thy misprision must perforce ensue   90
Some true love turned, and not a false turned true.

PUCK.   Then fate o'erules, that, one man holding troth,   92
A million fail, confounding oath on oath.   93

OBERON.   About the wood go swifter than the wind,
And Helena of Athens look thou find.
All fancy-sick she is and pale of cheer   96
With sighs of love, that costs the fresh blood dear.
By some illusion see thou bring her here.
I'll charm his eyes against she do appear.

PUCK.   I go, I go; look how I go,
Swifter than arrow from the Tartar's bow.

Exit.

OBERON.   *(Putting love juice in Demetrius' eyes)*
Flower of this purple dye,
Hit with Cupid's archery,
Sink in apple of his eye.   104
When his love he doth espy,
Let her shine as gloriously
As the Venus of the sky.
When thou wak'st, if she be by,
Beg of her for remedy.

Enter PUCK.

PUCK.   Captain of our fairy band,
Helena is here at hand,
And the youth, mistook by me,
Pleading for a lover's fee.   113
Shall we their fond pageant see?
Lord, what fools these mortals be!

OBERON.   Stand aside. The noise they make
Will cause Demetrius to awake.

133   **tales**   lies.

141   **Taurus**   mountain range in Asia.

142   **Turns to a crow**   seems black (in contrast to your white hand).

PUCK.   Then will two at once woo one;
       That must needs be sport alone;
       And those things do best please me
       That befall preposterously.

Enter LYSANDER *and* HELENA.

LYSANDER.   Why should you think that I should woo in
    scorn?
    Scorn and derision never come in tears.
  Look, when I vow, I weep; and vows so born,
    In their nativity all truth appears.
  How can these things in me seem scorn to you,
  Bearing the badge of faith, to prove them true?

HELENA.   You do advance your cunning more and more.
    When truth kills truth, O devilish-holy fray!
  These vows are Hermia's. Will you give her o'er?
    Weigh oath with oath, and you will nothing weigh.
  Your vows to her and me, put in two scales,
  Will even weigh; and both as light as tales.   133

LYSANDER.   I had no judgment when to her I swore.

HELENA.   Nor none, in my mind, now you give her o'er.

LYSANDER.   Demetrius loves her, and he loves not you.

DEMETRIUS.   (*Awaking*) O Helen, goddess, nymph,
    pefect, divine!
  To what, my love, shall I compare thine eyne?
  Crystal is muddy. O, how ripe in show
  Thy lips, those kissing cherries, tempting grow!
  That pure congealèd white, high Taurus' snow,   141
  Fanned with the eastern wind, turns to a crow   142
  When thou hold'st up thy hand. O, let me kiss
  This princess of pure white, this seal of bliss!

HELENA.   O spite! O hell! I see you all are bent
  To set against me for your merriment.
  If you were civil and knew courtesy,
  You would not do me thus much injury.
  Can you not hate me, as I know you do,
  But you must join in souls to mock me too?

157   **trim**   nice, fine (said sarcastically).

160   **extort**   twist, turn.

169   **I will none**   that is, I want no part of her.

175   **aby**   (əbī') pay for.

If you were men, as men you are in show,
You would not use a gentle lady so;
To vow, and swear, and superpraise my parts,
When I am sure you hate me with your hearts.
You both are rivals, and love Hermia,
And now both rivals, to mock Helena.
A trim exploit, a manly enterprise,   157
To conjure tears up in a poor maid's eyes
With your derision! None of noble sort
Would so offend a virgin and extort   160
A poor soul's patience, all to make you sport.

LYSANDER.   You are unkind, Demetrius. Be not so.
For you love Hermia; this you know I know.
And here, with all good will, with all my heart,
In Hermia's love I yield you up my part;
And yours of Helena to me bequeath,
Whom I do love, and will do till my death.

HELENA.   Never did mockers waste more idle breath.

DEMETRIUS.   Lysander, keep thy Hermia; I will none.   169
If e'er I loved her, all that love is gone.
My heart to her but as guestwise sojourned,
And now to Helen is it home returned,
There to remain.

LYSANDER.   Helen, it is not so.

DEMETRIUS.   Disparage not the faith thou dost not
    know,
Lest, to thy peril, thou aby it dear.   175
Look, where thy love comes; yonder is thy dear.

Enter HERMIA.

HERMIA.   Dark night, that from the eye his function
    takes,
The ear more quick of apprehension makes;
Wherein it doth impair the seeing sense,
It pays the hearing double recompense.
Thou are not by mine eye, Lysander, found;

187   **engilds**   gilds, brightens.

188   **oes**   small, circular spangles; here, the stars.

194   **in spite of me**   to vex me.

198   **counsel**   confidences.

203   **artificial**   skilled in artifice or creation.

204–205 **Have . . . sampler**   that is, they worked together to stitch a flower on a piece of embroidered cloth (sampler), or they worked on identical samplers.

208   **incorporate**   (in kôr'pərit) of one body.

211   **lovely**   loving.

213–214 **Two . . . crest**   two bodies, like a coat of arms that appears twice on a shield but is topped by one crest.

Mine ear, I thank it, brought me to thy sound.
But why unkindly didst thou leave me so?

LYSANDER.   Why should he stay, whom love doth press
    to go?

HERMIA.   What love could press Lysander from my side?

LYSANDER.   Lysander's love, that would not let him
    bide —
Fair Helena, who more engilds the night   187
Than all yon fiery oes and eyes of light.   188
Why seek'st thou me? Could not this make thee
    know,
The hate I bare thee made me leave thee so?

HERMIA.   You speak not as you think. It cannot be.

HELENA.   Lo, she is one of this confederacy!
Now I perceive they have conjoined all three
To fashion this false sport, in spite of me.   194
Injurious Hermia, most ungrateful maid!
Have you conspired, have you with these contrived
To bait me with this foul derision?
Is all the counsel that we two have shared,   198
The sisters' vows, the hours that we have spent,
When we have chid the hasty-footed time
For parting us — O, is all forgot?
All schooldays' friendship, childhood innocence?
We, Hermia, like two artificial gods,   203
Have with our needles created both one flower,   204
Both on one sampler, sitting on one cushion,
Both warbling of one song, both in one key,
As if our hands, our sides, voices, and minds,
Had been incorporate. So we grew together,   208
Like to a double cherry, seeming parted,
But yet an union in partition,
Two lovely berries molded on one stem;   211
So, with two seeming bodies, but one heart;
Two of the first, like coats in heraldry,   213
Due but to one, and crownèd with one crest.
And will you rent our ancient love asunder,

232   **grace** favor.

242   **argument** subject for a joke.

248   **If she cannot entreat** if Hermia cannot succeed by appealing.

To join with men in scorning your poor friend?
It is not friendly, 'tis not maidenly.
Our sex, as well as I, may chide you for it,
Though I alone do feel the injury.

HERMIA.   I am amazed at your passionate words.
I scorn you not. It seems that you scorn me.

HELENA.   Have you not set Lysander, as in scorn,
To follow me and praise my eyes and face?
And made your other love, Demetrius,
Who even but now did spurn me with his foot,
To call me goddess, nymph, divine, and rare,
Precious, celestial? Wherefore speaks he this
To her he hates? And wherefore doth Lysander
Deny your love, so rich within his soul,
And tender me, forsooth, affection,
But by your setting on, by your consent?
What though I be not so in grace as you,   232
So hung upon with love, so fortunate,
But miserable most, to love unloved?
This you should pity rather than despise.

HERMIA.   I understand not what you mean by this.

HELENA.   Ay, do. Persever, counterfeit sad looks,
Make mouths upon me when I turn my back,
Wink each at other, hold the sweet jest up.
This sport, well carried, shall be chronicled.
If you have any pity, grace, or manners,
You would not make me such an argument.   242
But fare ye well. 'Tis partly my own fault,
Which death or absence soon shall remedy.

LYSANDER.   Stay, gentle Helena; hear my excuse,
My love, my life, my soul, fair Helena!

HELENA.   O excellent!

HERMIA.   (To LYSANDER) Sweet, do not scorn her so.

DEMETRIUS.   (To LYSANDER) If she cannot entreat, I can
     compel.   248

257 **Ethiope** a reference to Hermia's dark hair and complexion.

258 **take on as** act as if.

LYSANDER.   Thou canst compel no more than she
    entreat.
  Thy threats have no more strength than her weak
    prayers.
  Helen, I love thee; by my life, I do!
  I swear by that which I will lose for thee,
  To prove him false that says I love thee not.

DEMETRIUS.   I say I love thee more than he can do.

LYSANDER.   If thou say so, withdraw, and prove it too.

DEMETRIUS.   Quick, come!

HERMIA.   Lysander, whereto tends all this?

LYSANDER.   Away, you Ethiope!

DEMETRIUS.   No, no, he'll   257
  Seem to break loose; take on as you would follow,   258
  But yet come not. You are a tame man, go!

LYSANDER.   (To HERMIA) Hang off, thou cat, thou burr!
  Vile thing, let loose,
  Or I will shake thee from me like a serpent!

HERMIA.   Why are you grown so rude? What change is
    this,
  Sweet love?

LYSANDER.   Thy love! Out, tawny Tartar, out!
  Out, loathèd med'cine! O hated potion, hence!

HERMIA.   Do you not jest?

HELENA.   Yes, sooth, and so do you.

LYSANDER.   Demetrius, I will keep my word with thee.

DEMETRIUS.   I would I had your bond, for I perceive
  A weak bond holds you. I'll not trust your word.

LYSANDER.   What, should I hurt her, strike her, kill her
    dead?
  Although I hate her, I'll not harm her so.

HERMIA.   What, can you do me greater harm than hate?
  Hate me! Wherefore? O me, what news, my love?
  Am not I Hermia? Are not you Lysander?

282   **canker-blossom**   worm that destroys a flower bud.

300   **curst**   shrewish, quarrelsome.

302   **right**   true.

I am as fair now as I was erewhile.
Since night you loved me; yet since night you left me.
Why, then you left me, — O, the gods forbid! —
In earnest, shall I say?

LYSANDER.   Ay, by my life!
And never did desire to see thee more.
Therefore be out of hope, of question, of doubt;
Be certain, nothing truer. 'Tis no jest
That I do hate thee and love Helena.

HERMIA.   (To HELENA) O me! You juggler! You
   canker-blossom!   282
You thief of love! What, have you come by night
And stol'n my love's heart from him?

HELENA.   Fine, i' faith!
Have you no modesty, no maiden shame,
No touch of bashfulness? What, will you tear
Impatient answers from my gentle tongue?
Fie, fie! You counterfeit, you puppet, you!

HERMIA.   Puppet? Why so? Ay, that way goes the game.
Now I perceive that she hath made compare
Between our statures; she hath urged her height,
And with her personage, her tall personage,
Her height, forsooth, she hath prevailed with him.
And are you grown so high in his esteem
Because I am so dwarfish and so low?
How low am I, thou painted maypole? Speak!
How low am I? I am not yet so low
But that my nails can reach unto thine eyes.

HELENA.   I pray you, though you mock me, gentlemen,
Let her not hurt me. I was never curst;   300
I have no gift at all in shrewishness;
I am a right maid for my cowardice.   302
Let her not strike me. You perhaps may think,
Because she is something lower than myself,
That I can match her.

HERMIA.   Lower? Hark, again!

314   **so**   if only.

323   **keen**   fierce

329   **knotgrass**   weed used in herbal medicine, formerly thought to stunt one's growth.

333   **intend**   give sign of.

335   **aby**   pay for.

HELENA.   Good Hermia, do not be so bitter with me.
I evermore did love you, Hermia,
Did ever keep your counsels, never wronged you;
Save that, in love unto Demetrius,
I told him of your stealth unto this wood.
He followed you; for love I followed him;
But he hath chid me hence, and threatened me
To strike me, spurn me, nay, to kill me too.
And now, so you will let me quiet go,   314
To Athens will I bear my folly back,
And follow you no further. Let me go.
You see how simple and how fond I am.

HERMIA.   Why, get you gone. Who is 't that hinders
you?

HELENA.   A foolish heart, that I leave here behind.

HERMIA.   What, with Lysander?

HELENA.   With Demetrius.

LYSANDER.   Be not afraid; she shall not harm thee,
Helena.

DEMETRIUS.   No, sir, she shall not, though you take her
part.

HELENA.   O, when she is angry, she is keen and shrewd.   323
She was a vixen when she went to school;
And though she be but little, she is fierce.

HERMIA.   "Little" again? Nothing but "low" and "little"?
Why will you suffer her to flout me thus?
Let me come to her.

LYSANDER.   Get you gone, you dwarf!
You minimus, of hindering knotgrass made!   329
You bead, you acorn.

DEMETRIUS.   You are too officious
In her behalf that scorns your services.
Let her alone. Speak not of Helena;
Take not her part. For, if thou dost intend   333
Never so little show of love to her,
Thou shalt aby it.   335

338   **cheek by jowl**   side by side.

339   **coil is 'long of you**   turmoil is on account of you.

352   **sort**   turn out.

356   **welkin**   sky.

357   **Acheron**   (ak'ə ron) river of Hades, the underworld.

LYSANDER.   Now she holds me not.
  Now follow, if thou dar'st, to try whose right,
  Of thine or mine, is most in Helena.

DEMETRIUS.   Follow? Nay, I'll go with thee, cheek by
    jowl.   338

                 Exeunt LYSANDER *and* DEMETRIUS.

HERMIA.   You, mistress, all this coil is 'long of you;   339
  Nay, go not back.

HELENA.   I will not trust you, I,
  Nor longer stay in your curst company.
  Your hands than mine are quicker for a fray.
  My legs are longer, though, to run away.

                                Exit.

HERMIA.   I am amazed, and know not what to say.

                                Exit.

OBERON.   (*To* PUCK) This is thy negligence. Still thou
    mistak'st,
  Or else committ'st thy knaveries willfully.

PUCK.   Believe me, king of shadows, I mistook.
  Did not you tell me I should know the man
  By the Athenian garments he had on?
  And so far blameless proves my enterprise,
  That I have 'nointed an Athenian's eyes;
  And so far am I glad it so did sort,   352
  As this their jangling I esteem a sport.

OBERON.   Thou seest these lovers seek a place to fight.
  Hie therefore, Robin, overcast the night;
  The starry welkin cover thou anon   356
  With drooping fog as black as Acheron,   357
  And lead these testy rivals so astray
  As one come not within another's way.
  Like to Lysander sometimes frame thy tongue,
  Then stir Demetrius up with bitter wrong;
  And sometimes rail thou like Demetrius.
  And from each other look thou lead them thus,

366   **this herb**   the antidote to love-in-idleness.

369   **wonted**   accustomed, usual.

370   **derision**   cause for laughter.

380   **Aurora's harbinger**   the morning star. Aurora was the Roman goddess of dawn.

387   **for aye**   forever.

389   **Morning's love**   Cephalus, a hunter loved by Aurora.

399   **Goblin**   Puck himself.

Till o'er their brows death-counterfeiting sleep
With leaden legs and batty wings doth creep.
Then crush this herb into Lysander's eye, 366
Whose liquor hath this virtuous property,
To take from thence all error with his might
And make his eyeballs roll with wonted sight. 369
When they next wake, all this derision 370
Shall seem a dream and fruitless vision,
And back to Athens shall the lovers wend
With league whose date till death shall never end.
Whiles I in this affair do thee employ,
I'll to my queen and beg her Indian boy;
And then I will her charmèd eye release
From monster's view, and all things shall be peace.

PUCK.   My fairy lord, this must be done with haste,
For night's swift dragons cut the clouds full fast,
And yonder shines Aurora's harbinger, 380
At whose approach, ghosts, wand'ring here and there,
Troop home to churchyards; damnèd spirits all,
That in crossways and floods have burial,
Already to their wormy beds are gone.
For fear lest day should look their shames upon,
They willfully themselves exile from light,
And must for aye consort with black-browed night. 387

OBERON.   But we are spirits of another sort.
I with the Morning's love have oft made sport, 389
And, like a forester, the groves may tread
Even till the eastern gate, all fiery red,
Opening on Neptune with fair blessèd beams,
Turns into yellow gold his salt green streams.
But notwithstanding, haste, make no delay.
We may effect this business yet ere day.

Exit.

PUCK.   Up and down, up and down,
I will lead them up and down.
I am feared in field and town.
Goblin, lead them up and down. 399
Here comes one.

402   **drawn**   with sword drawn.

409   **recreant**   coward.

412   **try**   test.

Enter LYSANDER.

LYSANDER.   Where art thou, proud Demetrius? Speak
thou now.

PUCK.   Here, villain, drawn and ready. Where art thou?   402

LYSANDER.   I will be with thee straight.

PUCK.   Follow me, then,
To plainer ground.

                    Exit LYSANDER, *following the voice.*

Enter DEMETRIUS.

DEMETRIUS.   Lysander! Speak again!
Thou runaway, thou coward, art thou fled?
Speak! In some bush? Where dost thou hide thy
head?

PUCK.   Thou coward, art thou bragging to the stars,
Telling the bushes that thou look'st for wars,
And wilt not come? Come, recreant; come, thou
child;   409
I'll whip thee with a rod. He is defiled
That draws a sword on thee.

DEMETRIUS.   Yea, art thou there?

PUCK.   Follow my voice. We'll try no manhood here.   412

                    Exeunt.

Enter LYSANDER.

LYSANDER.   He goes before me and still dares me on.
When I come where he calls, then he is gone.
The villain is much lighter-heeled than I.
I followed fast, but faster he did fly,
That fallen am I in dark uneven way,
And here will rest me. (*Lies down.*) Come, thou gentle
day!
For if but once thou show me thy gray light,
I'll find Demetrius, and revenge this spite.

                    (*Sleeps.*)

422   **Abide me**   face me; **wot**   know.

432   **Abate**   shorten.

439   **curst**   ill-tempered.

Enter PUCK *and* DEMETRIUS.

PUCK.   Ho, ho, ho! Coward, why com'st thou not?

DEMETRIUS.   Abide me, if thou dar'st; for well I wot   422
Thou runn'st before me, shifting every place,
And dar'st not stand, nor look me in the face.
Where art thou now?

PUCK.   Come hither. I am here.

DEMETRIUS.   Nay, then, thou mock'st me. Thou shalt
    buy this dear,
If ever I thy face by daylight see.
Now go thy way. Faintness constraineth me
To measure out my length on this cold bed.
By day's approach look to be visited.
                         (*Lies down and sleeps.*)

Enter HELENA.

HELENA.   O weary night, O long and tedious night,
Abate thy hours! Shine comforts from the east,   432
That I may back to Athens by daylight
From these that my poor company detest;
And sleep, that sometimes shuts up sorrow's eye,
Steal me awhile from mine own company.
                         (*Lies down and sleeps.*)

PUCK.   Yet but three? Come one more;
Two of both kinds makes up four.
Here she comes, curst and sad.   439
Cupid is a knavish lad,
Thus to make poor females mad.

Enter HERMIA.

HERMIA.   Never so weary, never so in woe,
Bedabbled with the dew, and torn with briers;
I can no further crawl, no further go;
My legs can keep no pace with my desires.
Here will I rest me till the break of day.
Heavens shield Lysander, if they mean a fray!
                         (*Lies down and sleeps.*)

Notes

PUCK.   On the ground
      Sleep sound.
      I'll apply
      To your eye,
   Gentle lover, remedy.
               (*Squeezing the juice on* LYSANDER'S *eye.*)
      When thou wak'st,
      Thou tak'st
      True delight
      In the sight
      Of thy former lady's eye;
      And the country proverb known,
      That every man should take his own,
      In your waking shall be shown:
      Jack shall have Jill;
      Naught shall go ill;
 The man shall have his mare again, and all shall be
   well.

                     Exit.

A MIDSUMMER NIGHT'S DREAM

ACT IV

" I have a reasonable good ear in music.
Let's have the tongs and the bones."

2   **coy**   caress.

SCENE 1

Titania, still enamoured of Bottom, lies down to sleep beside him. Oberon, coming upon the two, now tells Puck that he begins to pity Titania and that she has given up her changeling to him. He squeezes an herb into her eyes that will make her as she was before and tells Puck to remove the ass's head from Bottom. When Titania awakes, she and Oberon are reconciled. Theseus, Hippolyta, and Egeus find Lysander, Hermia, and Demetrius asleep. When the young people awake, Lysander is once more in love with Hermia, and Demetrius realizes that he loves Helena again. Theseus now declares that there will be three weddings.

The same.

LYSANDER, DEMETRIUS, HELENA, *and* HERMIA, *lying asleep.*

Enter TITANIA *and* BOTTOM; PEASEBLOSSOM, COBWEB, MOTH, MUSTARDSEED, *and other* FAIRIES *attending; and* OBERON *behind them.*

TITANIA.   Come, sit thee down upon this flowery bed,
    While I thy amiable cheeks do coy,   2
And stick musk roses in thy sleek smooth head,
    And kiss thy fair large ears, my gentle joy.

BOTTOM.   Where's Peaseblossom?

PEASEBLOSSOM.   Ready.

BOTTOM.   Scratch my head, Peaseblossom. Where's Mounsieur Cobweb?

COBWEB.   Ready.

BOTTOM.   Mounsieur Cobweb, good mounsieur, get you your weapons in your hand, and kill me a red-hipped humble-bee on the top of a thistle; and, good mounsieur, bring me the honey bag. Do not fret yourself too much in the action, mounsieur; and, good mounsieur, have a care the honey bag break not; I would be loath to have you overflown with a honey bag, signior. Where's Mounsieur Mustardseed?

MUSTARDSEED.   Ready.

20   **neaf**   fist.

24   **Cavalery Cobweb to scratch**   Bottom means "Cavalier," a
         form of address to a gentleman. Since Peaseblossom has
         been asked to scratch his head, the reference to Cobweb,
         who has been sent to get honey, is probably an error.

31   **tongs . . . bones**   rustic music made by tongs (an
         implement consisting of two pieces of wood or metal
         fastened together at one end and used for holding or lifting
         something) and bones, which were held between the
         fingers and used as clappers.

33   **peck of provender**   one-quarter bushel of grain.

35   **bottle**   bundle.

36   **fellow**   equal.

41   **exposition of**   disposition to.

BOTTOM.   Give me your neaf, Mounsieur Mustardseed.   20
Pray you, leave your courtesy, good mounsieur.

MUSTARDSEED.   What's your will?

BOTTOM.   Nothing, good mounsieur, but to help
Cavalery Cobweb to scratch. I must to the barber's,   24
mounsieur, for methinks I am marvelous hairy
about the face; and I am such a tender ass, if my
hair do but tickle me, I must scratch.

TITANIA.   What, wilt thou hear some music, my sweet
love?

BOTTOM.   I have a reasonable good ear in music. Let's
have the tongs and the bones.   31
                    (*Music: tongs, rural music*)

TITANIA.   Or say, sweet love, what thou desirest to eat.

BOTTOM.   Truly, a peck of provender. I could munch   33
your good dry oats. Methinks I have a great desire
to a bottle of hay. Good hay, sweet hay, hath no   35
fellow.   36

TITANIA.   I have a venturous fairy that shall seek the
squirrel's hoard, and fetch thee new nuts.

BOTTOM.   I had rather have a handful or two of dried
peas. But, I pray you, let none of your people stir
me. I have an exposition of sleep come upon me.   41

TITANIA.   Sleep thou, and I will wind thee in my arms.
Fairies, be gone, and be all ways away.
                    Exeunt FAIRIES.
So doth the woodbine the sweet honeysuckle
Gently entwist; the female ivy so
Enrings the barky fingers of the elm.
Oh, how I love thee! How I dote on thee!
                    (*They sleep.*)

                    Enter PUCK.

OBERON.   (*Advancing*) Welcome, good Robin. Seest
thou this sweet sight?

111

68   **other**   the four lovers.

69   **repair**   return.

75   **Dian's bud**   the flower that undoes the effects of the love potion.

Her dotage now I do begin to pity.
For, meeting her of late behind the wood
Seeking sweet favors for this hateful fool,
I did upbraid her and fall out with her.
For she his hairy temples then had rounded
With coronet of fresh and fragrant flowers;
And that same dew, which sometime on the buds
Was wont to swell, like round and orient pearls,
Stood now within the pretty flowerets' eyes
Like tears that did their own disgrace bewail.
When I had at my pleasure taunted her,
And she in mild terms begged my patience,
I then did ask of her her changeling child,
Which straight she gave me, and her fairy sent
To bear him to my bower in Fairyland.
And now I have the boy, I will undo
This hateful imperfection of her eyes.
And, gentle Puck, take this transformèd scalp
From off the head of this Athenian swain,
That he, awaking when the other do,   68
May all to Athens back again repair,   69
And think no more of this night's accidents
But as the fierce vexation of a dream.
But first I will release the Fairy Queen.
 Be as thou wast wont to be;
 See as thou wast wont to see.
 Dian's bud o'er Cupid's flower   75
 Hath such force and blessèd power.
Now, my Titania, wake you, my sweet queen.

TITANIA. (*Awaking*) My Oberon! What visions have I
 seen!
Methought I was enamored of an ass.

OBERON. There lies your love.

TITANIA.   How came these things to pass?
 O, how mine eyes do loathe his visage now!

OBERON. Silence awhile. Robin, take off this head.
 Titania, music call, and strike more dead
 Than common sleep of all these five the sense.

98   **sad**   sober.

107   **observation**   observance to a May morning mentioned in Act I, Scene 1, line 167.

108   **vaward**   vanguard; that is, morning.

TITANIA.   Music, ho! Music, such as charmeth sleep!
                                    (*Music*)

PUCK.   (*Removing the ass's head*) Now, when thou
        wak'st, with thine own fool's eyes peep.

OBERON.   Sound, music! Come, my queen, take hands
        with me,
    And rock the ground whereon these sleepers be.
                                    (*They dance.*)
    Now thou and I are new in amity,
    And will tomorrow midnight solemnly
    Dance in Duke Theseus' house triumphantly,
    And bless it to all fair prosperity.
    There shall the pairs of faithful lovers be
    Wedded, with Theseus, all in jollity.

PUCK.   Fairy king, attend, and mark:
        I do hear the morning lark.

OBERON.   Then, my queen, in silence sad,   98
        Trip we after night's shade.
        We the globe can compass soon,
        Swifter than the wand'ring moon.

TITANIA.   Come, my lord, and in our flight,
        Tell me how it came this night,
        That I sleeping here was found
        With these mortals on the ground.
                                    Exeunt.
                                (*Horns within.*)
        Enter THESEUS, HIPPOLYTA, EGEUS, *and train.*
THESEUS.   Go, one of you, find out the forester,
    For now our observation is performed;   107
    And since we have the vaward of the day,   108
    My love shall hear the music of my hounds.
    Uncouple in the western valley; let them go.
    Dispatch, I say, and find the forester.
                            Exit an ATTENDANT.
    We will, fair queen, up to the mountain's top
    And mark the musical confusion
    Of hounds and echo in conjunction.

115   **Cadmus**   mythical founder of Thebes.

123   **flewed**   having hanging, fleshy sides of the upper lip, such as a bloodhound does; **sanded**   of sandy color.

125   **dewlapped**   having hanging folds of skin under the neck.

126   **in mouth**   in their various cries.

137   **in grace of our solemnity**   in honor of our wedding ceremony.

HIPPOLYTA.   I was with Hercules and Cadmus once   115
   When in a wood of Crete they bayed the bear
   With hounds of Sparta. Never did I hear
   Such gallant chiding; for, besides the groves,
   The skies, the fountains, every region near
   Seemed all one mutual cry. I never heard
   So musical a discord, such sweet thunder.

THESEUS.   My hounds are bred out of the Spartan kind,
   So flewed, so sanded; and their heads are hung   123
   With ears that sweep away the morning dew;
   Crook-kneed, and dewlapped like Thessalian bulls;   125
   Slow in pursuit, but matched in mouth like bells,   126
   Each under each. A cry more tuneable
   Was never holloed to, nor cheered with horn,
   In Crete, in Sparta, nor in Thessaly.
   Judge when you hear. But, soft! What nymphs are
     these?

EGEUS.   My lord, this is my daughter here asleep,
   And this, Lysander; this Demetrius is;
   This Helena, old Nedar's Helena.
   I wonder of their being here together.

THESEUS.   No doubt they rose up early to observe
   The rite of May, and, hearing our intent,
   Came here in grace of our solemnity.   137
   But speak, Egeus; is not this the day
   That Hermia should give answer of her choice?

EGEUS.   It is, my lord.

THESEUS.   Go bid the huntsmen awake them with their
   horns.
                    Exit an ATTENDANT.
Horns and shout within. LYSANDER, DEMETRIUS, HELENA,
       and HERMIA *wake and start up.*
   Good morrow, friends. Saint Valentine is past.
   Begin these woodbirds but to couple now?

LYSANDER.   Pardon, my lord.
                     (They kneel.)

156   **Without**   beyond.

170   **idle gaud**   worthless trinket.

THESEUS.   I pray you all, stand up.

                                              (*They stand.*)

I know you two are rival enemies;
How comes this gentle concord in the world,
That hatred is so far from jealousy
To sleep by hate and fear no enmity?

LYSANDER.   My lord, I shall reply amazedly,
Half sleep, half waking; but as yet, I swear,
I cannot truly say how I came here.
But, as I think—for truly would I speak,
And now I do bethink me, so it is—
I came with Hermia hither. Our intent
Was to be gone from Athens, where we might,
Without the peril of the Athenian law—   156

EGEUS.   Enough, enough, my lord; you have enough.
I beg the law, the law, upon his head.
They would have stol'n away; they would, Demetrius,
Thereby to have defeated you and me,
You of your wife and me of my consent,
Of my consent that she should be your wife.

DEMETRIUS.   My lord, fair Helen told me of their
        stealth,
Of this their purpose hither to this wood,
And I in fury hither followed them,
Fair Helena in fancy following me.
But, my good lord, I wot not by what power—
But by some power it is—my love to Hermia,
Melted as the snow, seems to me now
As the remembrance of an idle gaud   170
Which in my childhood I did dote upon;
And all the faith, the virtue of my heart,
The object and the pleasure of mine eye,
Is only Helena. To her, my lord,
Was I betrothed ere I saw Hermia,
But, like a sickness, did I loathe this food;
But, as in health, come to my natural taste,
Now I do wish it, love it, long for it,
And will for evermore be true to it.

185   **for**   since.

192   **with parted eye**   out of focus.

207   **God's**   may God save.

THESEUS.   Fair lovers, you are fortunately met.
  Of this discourse we more will hear anon.
  Egeus, I will overbear your will;
  For in the temple, by and by, with us
  These couples shall eternally be knit.
  And, for the morning now is something worn,   185
  Our purposed hunting shall be set aside.
  Away with us to Athens! Three and three,
  We'll hold a feast in great solemnity.
  Come, Hippolyta.
             Exeunt THESEUS, HIPPOLYTA, *and train.*

DEMETRIUS.   These things seem small and
        undistinguishable,
  Like far-off mountains turnèd into clouds.

HERMIA   Methinks I see these things with parted eye,   192
  When every thing seems double.

HELENA.   So methinks;
  And I have found Demetrius like a jewel,
  Mine own, and not mine own.

DEMETRIUS.   Are you sure
  That we are awake? It seems to me
  That yet we sleep, we dream. Do not you think
  The Duke was here, and bid us follow him?

HERMIA.   Yea, and my father.

HELENA.   And Hippolyta.

LYSANDER.   And he did bid us follow to the temple.

DEMETRIUS.   Why, then, we are awake. Let's follow him,
  And by the way let us recount our dreams.
                                        Exeunt.

BOTTOM.   (*Awaking*) When my cue comes, call me, and
        I will answer. My next is, "Most fair Pyramus."
        Higho-ho! Peter Quince! Flute, the bellows-
        mender! Snout, the tinker! Starveling! God's my   207
        life, stolen hence, and left me asleep! I have had a
        most rare vision. I have had a dream, past the wit

214–216 **The eye of man . . . heart to report**   This is similar to
I Corinthians 2:9, but Bottom, as usual, has garbled it.

222   **her**   perhaps Thisbe's.

4   **transported**   carried off by fairies or transformed.

of man to say what dream it was. Man is but an ass
if he go about to expound this dream. Methought I
was—there is no man can tell what. Methought I
was—and methought I had—but man is but a
patched fool if he will offer to say what methought I
had. The eye of man hath not heard, the ear of
man hath not seen, man's hand is not able to taste,
his tongue to conceive, nor his heart to report,
what my dream was. I will get Peter Quince to
write a ballad of this dream. It shall be called
"Bottom's Dream," because it hath no bottom; and
I will sing it in the latter end of a play, before the
Duke. Peradventure, to make it the more gracious,
I shall sing it at her death.

214

222

Exit.

SCENE 2

*The rustics wonder what has become of Bottom and lament that the play cannot go on
without him. Bottom appears, however, and instructs them all to get ready to perform.*

Athens.

Enter QUINCE, FLUTE, SNOUT, *and* STARVELING.

QUINCE.   Have you sent to Bottom's house? Is he come
home yet?

STARVELING.   He cannot be heard of. Out of doubt he is
transported.

4

FLUTE.   If he come not, then the play is marred. It goes
not forward, doth it?

QUINCE.   It is not possible. You have not a man in all
Athens able to discharge Pyramus but he.

14   **a thing of naught**   a shameful thing.

36   **strings**   to attach the beards.

37   **pumps**   slippers.

39   **preferred**   selected for consideration.

FLUTE.   No, he hath simply the best wit of any
handicraft man in Athens.

QUINCE.   Yea, and the best person too, and he is a very
paramour for a sweet voice.

FLUTE.   You must say "paragon." A paramour is, God
bless us, a thing of naught.   14

Enter SNUG.

SNUG.   Masters, the Duke is coming from the temple,
and there is two or three lords and ladies more
married. If our sport had gone forward we had all
been made men.

FLUTE.   O sweet bully Bottom! Thus hath he lost
sixpence a day during his life; he could not have
scaped sixpence a day. An the Duke had not given
him sixpence a day for playing Pyramus, I'll be
hanged. He would have deserved it. Sixpence a day
in Pyramus, or nothing.

Enter BOTTOM.

BOTTOM.   Where are these lads? Where are these
hearts?

QUINCE.   Bottom! O most courageous day! O most
happy hour!

BOTTOM.   Masters, I am to discourse wonders; but ask
me not what. For if I tell you, I am no true
Athenian. I will tell you everything, right as it fell
out.

QUINCE.   Let us hear, sweet Bottom.

BOTTOM.   Not a word of me. All that I will tell you is
that the Duke hath dined. Get your apparel
together, good strings to your beards, new ribbons   36
to your pumps; meet presently at the palace; every   37
man look o'er his part; for the short and the long is,
our play is preferred. In any case, let Thisbe have   39

Notes

clean linen; and let not him that plays the lion pare his nails, for they shall hang out for the lion's claws. And, most dear actors, eat no onions nor garlic, for we are to utter sweet breath; and I do not doubt but to hear them say it is a sweet comedy. No more words. Away! Go, away!

Exeunt.

A MIDSUMMER NIGHT'S DREAM

ACT V

"Here come the lovers, full of joy and mirth."

8   **compact**   formed.

11   **brow of Egypt**   face of a gypsy.

SCENE 1

Theseus chooses to see the play of Pyramus and Thisbe, and it is performed, to occasional jesting remarks from the audience. Theseus is kind in his appreciation of the play, however. When all have gone to bed, Puck enters to sweep, and Oberon, Titania, and the fairies bless the three couples and their future offspring. Puck delivers a short speech to the audience suggesting that if the play has offended them, they should pretend that they have slept and dreamed.

Athens. The palace of THESEUS.

Enter THESEUS, HIPPOLYTA, PHILOSTRATE, LORDS,
and ATTENDANTS.

HIPPOLYTA.   'Tis strange, my Theseus, that these lovers
  speak of.

THESEUS.   More strange than true. I never may believe
  These antique fables nor these fairy toys.
  Lovers and madmen have such seething brains,
  Such shaping fantasies, that apprehend
  More than cool reason ever comprehends.
  The lunatic, the lover, and the poet
  Are of imagination all compact.   8
  One sees more devils than vast hell can hold,
  That is the madman. The lover, all as frantic,
  Sees Helen's beauty in a brow of Egypt.   11
  The poet's eye, in a fine frenzy rolling,
  Doth glance from heaven to earth, from earth to
    heaven;
  And as imagination bodies forth
  The forms of things unknown, the poet's pen
  Turns them to shapes, and gives to airy nothing
  A local habitation and a name.
  Such tricks hath strong imagination
  That, if it would but apprehend some joy,
  It comprehends some bringer of that joy;
  Or in the night, imagining some fear,
  How easy is a bush supposed a bear!

27   **admirable**   source of wonder.

32   **masques**   courtly entertainments.

42   **brief**   summary.

HIPPOLYTA.   But all the story of the night told over,
And all their minds transfigured so together,
More witnesseth than fancy's images
And grows to something of great constancy;
But, howsoever, strange and admirable.   27

Enter LYSANDER, DEMETRIUS, HERMIA, *and* HELENA.

THESEUS.   Here come the lovers, full of joy and mirth.
Joy, gentle friends! Joy and fresh days of love
Accompany your hearts!

LYSANDER.   More than to us
Wait in your royal walks, your board, your bed!

THESEUS.   Come now, what masques, what dances shall
    we have,   32
To wear away this long age of three hours
Between our after-supper and bedtime?
Where is our usual manager of mirth?
What revels are in hand? Is there no play
To ease the anguish of a torturing hour?
Call Philostrate.

PHILOSTRATE.   Here, mighty Theseus.

THESEUS.   Say, what abridgment have you for this
    evening?
What masque? What music? How shall we beguile
The lazy time, if not with some delight?

PHILOSTRATE.   There is a brief how many sports are
    ripe.   42
Make choice of which your Highness will see first.
                        (*Giving him a paper.*)

THESEUS.   (*Reads*) "The battle with the Centaurs, to be
    sung
By an Athenian eunuch to the harp."
We'll none of that. That have I told my love,
In glory of my kinsman Hercules.
(*Reads*) "The riot of the tipsy Bacchanals,
Tearing the Thracian singer in their rage."   .
That is an old device; and it was played

55   **sorting with**   appropriate to.

74   **unbreathed**   unexercised.

80   **stretched and conned**   strained and memorized.

When I from Thebes came last a conqueror.
(*Reads*) "The thrice three Muses mourning for the
    death
Of Learning, late deceased in beggary."
That is some satire, keen and critical,
Not sorting with a nuptial ceremony.   55
(*Reads*) "A tedious brief scene of young Pyramus
And his love Thisbe; very tragical mirth."
Merry and tragical? Tedious and brief?
That is, hot ice and wondrous strange snow.
How shall we find the concord of this discord?

PHILOSTRATE.   A play there is, my lord, some ten words
    long,
Which is as brief as I have known a play;
But by ten words, my lord, it is too long,
Which makes it tedious. For in all the play
There is not one word apt, one player fitted.
And tragical, my noble lord, it is,
For Pyramus therein doth kill himself.
Which, when I saw rehearsed, I must confess,
Made mine eyes water; but more merry tears
The passion of loud laughter never shed.

THESEUS.   What are they that do play it?

PHILOSTRATE.   Hardhanded men that work in Athens
    here,
Which never labored in their minds till now,
And now have toiled their unbreathed memories   74
With this same play, against your nuptial.

THESEUS.   And we will hear it.

PHILOSTRATE.   No, my noble lord,
It is not for you. I have heard it over,
And it is nothing, nothing in the world;
Unless you can find sport in their intents,
Extremely stretched and conned with cruel pain,   80
To do you service.

THESEUS.   I will hear that play;
For never anything can be amiss

92   **Takes . . . merit**   values it for the effort made rather than for the good effect.

93   **clerks**   learned men.

106   **Prologue**   speaker of the prologue.

When simpleness and duty tender it.
Go, bring them in, and take your places, ladies.

Exit PHILOSTRATE.

HIPPOLYTA.   I love not to see wretchedness o'ercharged,
And duty in his service perishing.

THESEUS.   Why, gentle sweet, you shall see no such
thing.

HIPPOLYTA.   He says they can do nothing in this kind.

THESEUS.   The kinder we, to give them thanks for
nothing.
Our sport shall be to take what they mistake;
And what poor duty cannot do, noble respect
Takes it in might, not merit.   92
Where I have come, great clerks have purposèd   93
To greet me with premeditated welcomes;
Where I have seen them shiver and look pale,
Make periods in the midst of sentences,
Throttle their practiced accent in their fears,
And, in conclusion, dumbly have broke off,
Not paying me a welcome. Trust me, sweet,
Out of this silence yet I picked a welcome;
And in the modesty of fearful duty
I read as much as from the rattling tongue
Of saucy and audacious eloquence.
Love, therefore, and tongue-tied simplicity
In least speak most, to my capacity.

Enter PHILOSTRATE.

PHILOSTRATE.   So please your Grace, the Prologue is
addressed.   106

THESEUS.   Let him approach.

(*Flourish of trumpets.*)
Enter QUINCE, *the* PROLOGUE.

PROLOGUE.   If we offend, it is with our good will.
That you should think, we come not to offend,
But with good will. To show our simple skill,

118   **stand upon points**   pay attention to punctuation or worry about fine points.

124   **government**   control.

137   **think no scorn**   think it no disgraceful matter.

139   **hight**   is called.

That is the true beginning of our end.
Consider, then, we come but in despite.
     We do not come, as minding to content you,
Our true intent is. All for your delight,
     We are not here. That you should here repent you,
The actors are at hand; and, by their show,
You shall know all, that you are like to know.

THESEUS.   This fellow doth not stand upon points.   118

LYSANDER.   He hath rid his prologue like a rough colt;
     he knows not the stop. A good moral, my lord: it is
     not enough to speak, but to speak true.

HIPPOLYTA.   Indeed he hath played on his prologue like
     a child on a recorder: a sound, but not in
     government.   124

THESEUS.   He speech was like a tangled chain: nothing
     impaired, but all disordered. Who is next?

Enter PYRAMUS *and* THISBE, WALL, MOONSHINE, *and* LION.
PROLOGUE.   Gentles, perchance you wonder at this
          show;
     But wonder on, till truth make all things plain.
This man is Pyramus, if you would know;
     This beauteous lady Thisbe is certain.
This man, with lime and roughcast, doth present
     Wall, that vile Wall which did these lovers sunder;
And through Wall's chink, poor souls, they are
          content
     To whisper. At the which let no man wonder.
This man, with lantern, dog, and bush of thorn,
     Presenteth Moonshine; for, if you will know,
By moonshine did these lovers think no scorn   137
     To meet at Ninus' tomb, there, there to woo.
This grisly beast, which Lion hight by name,   139
The trusty Thisbe, coming first by night,
Did scare away, or rather did affright;
And, as she fled, her mantle she did fall,
     Which Lion vile with bloody mouth did stain.

147   **broached**   stabbed.

163   **right and sinister**   right and left; that is, horizontally.

Anon comes Pyramus, sweet youth and tall,
　And finds his trusty Thisbe's mantle slain:
Whereat, with blade, with bloody blameful blade,
　He bravely broached his boiling bloody breast: 147
And Thisbe, tarrying in mulberry shade,
　His dagger drew, and died. For all the rest,
Let Lion, Moonshine, Wall, and lovers twain
At large discourse, while here they do remain.
　　　　　Exeunt PROLOGUE, PYRAMUS, THISBE, LION,
　　　　　　　　　　　　and MOONSHINE.

THESEUS.　　I wonder if the lion be to speak.

DEMETRIUS.　　No wonder, my lord. One lion may, when
　many asses do.

WALL.　　In this same interlude it doth befall
That I, one Snout by name, present a wall;
And such a wall, as I would have you think,
That had in it a crannied hole or chink,
Through which the lovers, Pyramus and Thisbe,
Did whisper often very secretly.
This loam, this roughcast, and this stone doth show
That I am that same wall; the truth is so.
And this the cranny is, right and sinister, 163
Through which the fearful lovers are to whisper.

THESEUS.　　Would you desire lime and hair to speak
　better?

DEMETRIUS.　　It is the wittiest partition that ever I heard
　discourse, my lord.

THESEUS.　　Pyramus draws near the wall. Silence!

　　　　　　　Enter PYRAMUS.

PYRAMUS.　　O grim-looked night!O night with hue so
　black!
　O night, which ever art when day is not!
O night, O night! Alack, alack, alack,
　I fear my Thisbe's promise is forgot.
And thou, O wall, O sweet, O lovely wall,

141

182   **sensible**   capable of feeling.

197   **Limander**   mistake for Leander.

198   **Helen**   mistake for Hero. Hero and Leander were famous lovers.

199   **Shafalus to Procrus**   errors for Cephalus and Procris, also famous lovers.

That stand'st between her father's ground and
    mine,
Thou wall, O wall, O sweet and lovely wall,
    Show me thy chink, to blink through with mine
    eyne!
                (WALL *holds up his fingers to make a chink.*)
Thanks, courteous wall. Jove shield thee well for this.
    But what see I? No Thisbe do I see.
O wicked wall, through whom I see no bliss!
    Cursed be thy stones for thus deceiving me!

THESEUS.   The wall, methinks, being sensible, should
    curse again.   182

PYRAMUS.   No, in truth, sir, he should not. "Deceiving
    me" is Thisbe's cue: she is to enter now, and I am
    to spy her through the wall. You shall see, it will
    fall pat as I told you. Yonder she comes.

                    Enter THISBE.

THISBE.   O wall, full often hast thou heard my moans
    For parting my fair Pyramus and me.
My cherry lips have often kissed thy stones,
    Thy stones with lime and hair knit up in thee.

PYRAMUS.   I see a voice. Now will I to the chink,
To spy an I can hear my Thisbe's face.
Thisbe!

THISBE.   My love! Thou art my love, I think.

PYRAMUS.   Think what thou wilt, I am thy lover's grace,
    And like Limander am I trusty still.   197

THISBE.   And I like Helen, till the Fates me kill.   198

PYRAMUS.   Not Shafalus to Procrus was so true.   199

THISBE.   As Shafalus to Procrus, I to you.

PYRAMUS.   O, kiss me through the hole of this vile wall!

THISBE.   I kiss the wall's hole, not your lips at all.

PYRAMUS.   Wilt thou at Ninny's tomb meet me
    straightway?

205   **'Tide**   betide, come.

225   **lion fell**   fierce lion.

233   **goose . . . discretion**   as discreet or prudent as a goose; that is, silly.

THISBE. 'Tide life, 'tide death, I come without delay.   205
Exeunt PYRAMUS *and* THISBE.

WALL. Thus have I, Wall, my part dischargèd so;
And, being done, thus Wall away doth go.
Exit.

THESEUS. Now is the mural down between the two
neighbors.

DEMETRIUS. No remedy, my lord, when walls are so
willful to hear without warning.

HIPPOLYTA. This is the silliest stuff that ever I heard.

THESEUS. The best in this kind are but shadows; and
the worst are no worse, if imagination amend them.

HIPPOLYTA. It must be your imagination then, and not
theirs.

THESEUS. If we imagine no worse of them than they of
themselves, they may pass for excellent men. Here
come two noble beasts in, a man and a lion.

Enter LION *and* MOONSHINE.

LION. You, ladies, you, whose gentle hearts do fear
The smallest monstrous mouse that creeps on floor,
May now perchance both quake and tremble here,
When lion rough in wildest rage doth roar,
Then know that I, as Snug the joiner, am
A lion fell, nor else no lion's dam;   225
For, if I should as lion come in strife
Into this place, 'twere pity on my life.

THESEUS. A very gentle beast, and of a good
conscience.

DEMETRIUS. The very best at a beast, my lord, that e'er
I saw.

LYSANDER. This lion is a very fox for his valor.

THESEUS. True; and a goose for his discretion.   233

DEMETRIUS. Not so, my lord, for his valor cannot carry
his discretion, and the fox carries the goose.

145

241–242 **on his head**   as a sign that his wife has betrayed him.

251   **for**   because.

THESEUS.   His discretion, I am sure, cannot carry his
valor; for the goose carries not the fox. It is well.
Leave it to his discretion, and let us listen to the
moon.

MOON.   This lanthorn doth the hornèd moon present—

DEMETRIUS.   He should have worn the horns on his   241
head.

THESEUS.   He is no crescent, and his horns are invisible
within the circumference.

MOON.   This lanthorn doth the hornèd moon present;
Myself the man i' the moon do seem to be.

THESEUS.   This is the greatest error of all the rest. The
man should be put into the lantern. How is it else
the man i' the moon?

DEMETRIUS.   He dares not come there for the candle,
for you see, it is already in snuff.   251

HIPPOLYTA.   I am aweary of this moon. Would he would
change!

THESEUS.   It appears, by his small light of discretion,
that he is in the wane; but yet, in courtesy, in all
reason, we must stay the time.

LYSANDER.   Proceed, Moon.

MOON.   All that I have to say is to tell you that the
lanthorn is the moon; I, the man i' th' moon; this
thornbush, my thornbush; and this dog, my dog.

DEMETRIUS.   Why, all these should be in the lantern; for
all these are in the moon. But, silence! Here comes
Thisbe.

Enter THISBE.

THISBE.   This is old Ninny's tomb. Where is my love?

LION.   (*Roaring*) O!

(THISBE *runs off.*)

DEMETRIUS.   Well roared, Lion.

THESEUS.   Well run, Thisbe.

270   **moused** shaken, torn.

279   **dole** sorrowful event.

285   **Furies** avenging goddesses of Greek myth.

286   **Fates** the three goddesses of destiny in Greek myth who spin, draw, and cut the thread of life.

287   **thread and thrum,** literally, the warp (lengthwise threads) in weaving and the loose end of the warp; figuratively, the whole of anything, everything.

291   **Beshrew** blame.

HIPPOLYTA.   Well shone, Moon. Truly, the moon shines
   with a good grace.
                 (*The* LION *shakes* THISBE'S *mantle, and exits.*)

THESEUS.   Well moused, Lion.   270

DEMETRIUS.   And then came Pyramus.

LYSANDER.   And so the lion vanished.

                 Enter PYRAMUS.

PYRAMUS.   Sweet Moon, I thank thee for thy sunny
      beams;
      I thank thee, Moon, for shining now so bright;
   For, by thy gracious, golden, glittering gleams,
      I trust to take of truest Thisbe sight.
            But stay, O spite!
            But mark, poor knight,
   What dreadful dole is here?   279
            Eyes, do you see?
            How can it be?
   O dainty duck! O dear!
            Thy mantle good,
            What, stained with blood?
   Approach, ye Furies fell!   285
            O Fates, come, come,   286
            Cut thread and thrum;   287
   Quail, crush, conclude, and quell!

THESEUS.   This passion, and the death of a dear friend,
   would go near to make a man look sad.

HIPPOLYTA.   Beshrew my heart, but I pity the man.   291

PYRAMUS.   O wherefore, Nature, didst thou lions frame?
   Since lion vile hath here deflowered my dear,
   Which is — no, no — which was the fairest dame
      That lived, that loved, that liked, that looked with
         cheer.
            Come, tears, confound,
            Out, sword, and wound
   The pap of Pyramus;
            Ay, that left pap,

308   **No die, but an ace**   a pun on *die*. A die is one of a pair of dice, and an ace the side of a die with one spot. Demetrius thinks Bottom's performance is worth but an ace, not the whole die.

320   **mote**   small particle.

325   **videlicet**   (vi del'i sit) that is to say.

Where heart doth hop.

(Stabs himself.)

Thus die I, thus, thus, thus.
   Now am I dead,
   Now am I fled;
My soul is in the sky.
   Tongue, lose thy light;
   Moon, take thy flight.

Exit MOONSHINE.

Now die, die, die, die, die.

(Dies.)

DEMETRIUS.   No die, but an ace, for him; for he is but 308
   one.

LYSANDER.   Less than an ace, man; for he is dead; he is
   nothing.

THESEUS.   With the help of a surgeon he might yet
   recover, and prove an ass.

HIPPOLYTA.   How chance Moonshine is gone before
   Thisbe comes back and finds her lover?

THESEUS.   She will find him by starlight. Here she
   comes; and her passion ends the play.

Enter THISBE.

HIPPOLYTA.   Methinks she should not use a long one for
   such a Pyramus. I hope she will be brief.

DEMETRIUS.   A mote will turn the balance, which 320
   Pyramus, which Thisbe, is the better; he for a man,
   God warrant us; she for a woman, God bless us.

LYSANDER.   She hath spied him already with those
   sweet eyes.

DEMETRIUS.   And thus she means, videlicet: 325

THISBE.   Asleep, my love?
   What, dead, my dove?
    O Pyramus, arise!
    Speak, speak. Quite dumb?
    Dead, dead? A tomb

338   **Sisters Three** the Fates.

346   **imbrue** stain with blood.

355   **Bergomask dance** rustic dance.

Must cover thy sweet eyes.
    These lily lips,
    This cherry nose,
These yellow cowslip cheeks,
    Are gone, are gone:
    Lovers, make moan.
His eyes were green as leeks.
    O Sisters Three,   338
    Come, come to me,
With hands as pale as milk;
    Lay them in gore,
    Since you have shore
With shears his thread of silk.
    Tongue, not a word.
    Come, trusty sword;
Come, blade, my breast imbrue!   346

                                      (*Stabs herself.*)

    And, farewell, friends.
    Thus Thisbe ends.
Adieu, adieu, adieu.

                                                 (*Dies.*)

THESEUS.   Moonshine and Lion are left to bury the
    dead.

DEMETRIUS.   Ay, and Wall too.

BOTTOM.   (*Starting up*) No. I assure you; the wall is
    down that parted their fathers. Will it please you to
    see the epilogue, or to hear a Bergomask dance   355
    between two of our company?

THESEUS.   No epilogue, I pray you; for your play needs
    no excuse. Never excuse; for when the players are
    all dead, there need none to be blamed. Marry, if
    he that writ it had played Pyramus and hanged
    himself in Thisbe's garter, it would have been a fine
    tragedy; and so it is, truly, and very notably
    discharged. But, come, your Bergomask. Let your
    epilogue alone.

                                              (*A dance.*)

376   **fordone**   exhausted.

377   **wasted brands**   burned-out logs.

386   **triple Hecate's**   the goddess Hecate ruled in heaven, earth, and hell.

392   **sweep . . . door**   Either he was to sweep the dust from behind the door or sweep it behind the door where it would not show.

The iron tongue of midnight hath told twelve.
Lovers, to bed, 'tis almost fairy time.
I fear we shall outsleep the coming morn
As much as we this night have overwatched.
This palpable-gross play hath well beguiled
The heavy gait of night. Sweet friends, to bed.
A fortnight hold we this solemnity,
In nightly revels and new jollity.

Exeunt.

Enter PUCK *with a broom.*

PUCK.   Now the hungry lion roars,
    And the wolf behowls the moon;
Whilst the heavy ploughman snores,
    All with weary task fordone.   376
Now the wasted brands do glow,   377
    Whilst the screech owl, screeching loud,
Puts the wretch that lies in woe
    In remembrance of a shroud.
Now it is the time of night
    That the graves, all gaping wide,
Every one lets forth his sprite,
    In the church-way paths to glide.
And we fairies, that do run
    By the triple Hecate's team,   386
From the presence of the sun,
    Following darkness like a dream,
Now are frolic. Not a mouse
Shall disturb this hallowed house.
I am sent with broom before,
To sweep the dust behind the door.   392

Enter OBERON *and* TITANIA *with their train.*
OBERON.   Through the house give glimmering light,
    By the dead and drowsy fire;
Every elf and fairy sprite
    Hop as light as bird from brier;

399   **rehearse**   recite.

407   **create**   created.

417   **consecrate**   consecrated, sacred.

418   **take his gait**   go his way.

430   **a dream**   that is, "A Midsummer Night's Dream."

And this ditty, after me,
Sing, and dance it trippingly.

TITANIA.   First, rehearse your song by rote,   399
To each word a warbling note.
Hand in hand, with fairy grace,
Will we sing, and bless this place.

(*Song and dance.*)

OBERON.   Now, until the break of day,
Through this house each fairy stray.
To the best bride-bed will we,
Which by us shall blessèd be;
And the issue there create   407
Ever shall be fortunate.
So shall all the couples three
Ever true in loving be;
And the blots of Nature's hand
Shall not in their issue stand;
Never mole, harelip, nor scar,
Nor mark prodigious, such as are
Despisèd in nativity,
Shall upon their children be.
With this field dew consecrate,   417
Every fairy take his gait,   418
And each several chamber bless,
Through this palace, with sweet peace;
And the owner of it blest
Ever shall in safety rest.
Trip away; make no stay;
Meet me all by break of day.

Exeunt OBERON, TITANIA, *and train.*

PUCK.   (*To the audience*) If we shadows have offended,
Think but this, and all is mended,
That you have but slumbered here,
While these visions did appear.
And this weak and idle theme,
No more yielding but a dream,   430
Gentles, do not reprehend.
If you pardon, we will mend.

435   **serpent's tongue**   hissing.

439   **Give . . . hands**   applaud.

440   **restore amends**   give satisfaction in return.

And, as I am an honest Puck,
If we have unearnèd luck
Now to scape the serpent's tongue,   435
We will make amends ere long;
Else the Puck a liar call.
So, good night unto you all.
Give me your hands, if we be friends,   439
And Robin shall restore amends.   440

Exit.

Thinking About the Play

Act I

1. In the first three speeches of Scene 1, Theseus and Hippolyta set a tone for the whole play's approach to relationships between men and women. Try reading those first nineteen lines, once with Theseus in control, then with Hippolyta in charge. Compare your reactions with your classmates', come to a conclusion, and explain that conclusion in writing. By the end of the play, you will be able to decide what reactions you want from the audience and how to use this opening scene to prepare for it.

2. Lysander's statement, "The course of true love never did run smooth" (Scene 1, line 134) has become one of the most famous lines in the play. Can that "course" *ever* run smooth in a play or movie? In real life? After a short discussion, come to some conclusions and support them with at least two specific examples.

3. In Scene 1, Helena says, "Love looks not with the eyes but with the mind" (line 234). If she means that we fall in love with people's character rather than with their looks, doesn't she contradict herself in lines 238–239? How does her observation apply to her? To Demetrius? To you? Young people are often criticized for choosing boyfriends and girlfriends solely on the basis of physical appearance. Is the criticism justified?

4. Hippolyta has a small but important role in the play. In Scene 1, for example, she has only one short speech—at the very beginning. Write the stage directions for the actress playing her in this scene. Where should she stand, and what should she be doing during her lines? Where on the stage should she be until her exit, at line 127? Where should she move, and when? To what lines by other characters should she react, and how?

5. As the workmen begin to prepare their play (Scene 2), Nick Bottom misuses words, interrupts Peter Quince constantly, and tries to take every part he likes. But if the audience gets disgusted with him, the humor in his later scenes will turn bitter. What advice would you give to the actor playing Bottom to keep the character sympathetic while he's being foolish?

Act II

1. Puck's speech in Scene 1 about Oberon and Titania contains the information the audience needs to understand the couple's quarrel (lines 18–31). Titania gives her side of the story later in the scene (lines 121–137). What, exactly, is the problem? Playing the role of a counselor, propose a solution to the two.

2. In Scene 1, how does Titania say her quarrel with Oberon has affected nature and the people? The problems seem pretty severe; why, do you suppose, don't the Duke of Athens, the young lovers, or the "rude mechanicals" even mention them?

3. When he awakes and looks at Helena, Lysander says that "the will of man is by his reason swayed." What is ironic about this statement?

4. By the end of Act II, Shakespeare has begun to build sets of parallels among the worlds of this play. We have two adult couples to compare and contrast, three male leaders, and two young couples. Think of ways a director could call these parallels to an audience's attention.

5. Now that you've spent some time in the play's third "world," decide what kind of "wood" it should be. An English wood with hedges, graceful trees, and wildflowers? A more frightening forest of tall trees and heavy undergrowth that makes it difficult for the characters to walk? Another type of wood? (There is no "right" answer, but each would change the tone and feeling of the play.)

Act III

1. What first worries Bottom and the other artisans about their play, and how do they propose to solve their problems?

2. How do they solve the problem of depicting moonshine and a wall? How would Shakespeare have solved this problem? How would you?

3. Bottom says that "reason and love keep little company together." What has attracted Titania to Bottom and how does her attraction contradict Helena's views on the nature of love? Which of the people in love have behaved "reasonably" so far in the play and which unreasonably?

4. The arguments among the lovers grow and cross, disintegrating into childish name-calling. What conclusions can the audience or reader draw about the "power of love" as Helena, Lysander, and Hermia each stoop to attacks on others' appearance rather than character?

5. How does Oberon dissociate himself from the night spirits Puck mentions in lines 381–388 of Scene 2, and why might he do so?

Act IV

1. Trace the lines and images that herald dawn, beginning with Puck's speech in Act III, line 378, and continuing into Act IV. If you were staging a modern production of this play, how would you indicate the approach of dawn to accompany these various lines?

2. The fairies have been aware of the lovers, but the lovers have not been aware of the fairies. What might be the reason for this?

3. The lovers and Bottom all seem to think they have dreamed the night's adventures, and Titania says, "What visions have I seen!" Do you think Shakespeare's intention was to portray a dreamlike experience? If so, what does this have to do with love? If not, what was his intention?

4. The actor playing Egeus has a difficult job. If Egeus were a silly fool (as he is sometimes played), Theseus would probably not have sided so strongly with him in Act I by threatening Hermia with death. How, then, should Egeus react when Theseus "overbears" his will at the end of Scene 1?

5. Which of these three elements of drama—plot, character, or setting—is most important to this play? Which is next important? Do you think this is typical of comedy? Be prepared to support your answer.

Act V

1. In one of the play's most lyrical speeches (Scene 1, lines 7–17), Theseus puts the lunatic, the lover, and the poet in the same category. Why? What is his opinion of poets? How does Hippolyta reply?

2. In commenting on the interlude, Theseus says, "The best in this kind are but shadows; and the worst are no worse, if imagination amend them." What does he mean? Explain how Shakespeare might mean the lines to apply to his own plays in general, and to *A Midsummer Night's Dream* in particular.

3. Hippolyta says, "It must be your imagination then, and not theirs." Does the Pyramus and Thisbe play leave anything to the imagination? What does this tell you about the nature of "successful" art?

Acts I–V

1. Bottom is transformed for awhile in the play, but the transformation does not change him in the same way it changes Lysander and Demetrius. What does this tell you about Bottom?

2. The theme of change is constant in this play. Trace this theme through all the references to change and tell what you think is the purpose of all these changes and transformations. Do you think the reader or audience is changed after encountering the play?

3. Is this a sexist play? If someone objected to producing this play on the grounds that it is sexist, what would you say?

Responding Through Writing

Act I

1. In a few paragraphs, characterize Theseus in this act. Study his lines, and, before beginning to write, think about his position in Athens, how he won Hippolyta, his feelings for her now, the contrast between him and Egeus, and his treatment of Hermia. Support your characterization with examples from the play and give line numbers for each.

Act II

1. Act II, Scene 1 has several "set pieces," speeches that have become famous and are often read or performed as separate poems. The best known are Puck's "I am that merry wanderer of the night" (lines 43–57), Titania's "His mother was a vot'ress" (lines 121–137), Oberon's "Cupid's fiery shaft" (lines 155–168) and "I know a bank" (lines 249–258). In a short but specific written exercise in close reading, analyze the language of one of these speeches. Concentrate on the images, the movement and pace, and the arrangement of the piece you choose.

2. Choose one of the sets of parallels in Thinking About the Play, Act II, question 4, for a short essay of comparison and contrast.

Act III

1. Act III deals repeatedly with violence. The "mechanicals" try to tone down, even to explain, the violence in their play. Helena quarrels with Lysander and with Hermia, and Hermia with Lysander. The act ends with Lysander and Demetrius trying to stage a physical fight. You could even argue that Oberon's meddling with the "juice" constitutes a form of emotional violence.

    Our word "essay" comes from a French verb that means "to try." Write a short essay in which you "try out" your ideas on violence in entertainment. Begin with your thoughts on Act III of *A Midsummer Night's Dream*, then explore your ideas on violence in one form of modern entertainment.

2. In Scene 2, Puck exclaims, "Lord, what fools these mortals be!" To what extent do you think the mortals in this act are fools? To what extent are Oberon and Puck to blame for the trouble? What could Shakespeare be using Puck and Oberon to represent, and what could that tell us about the source of some of our problems?

Act IV

1. The lovers are all sorted out now—or are they? Isn't Demetrius still under a spell? Did Shakespeare forget? Or is love a spell anyway so that it doesn't matter? Other logical curiosities have come up in the play; there's a May festival going on in "midsummer," for instance. Find one or two more illogical occurrences in the play. Then write a short essay in which you explain whether each matters or what Shakespeare might have had in mind.

Act V

1. Some claim that the behavior of the court members during the performance of "Pyramus and Thisbe" undermines their nobility. Do you think the nobles' comments should be tinged with humor? Disgust? Cruelty? Something else? How would each of these attitudes change the way an audience sees the nobles in this act? State and explain your conclusion in a short essay.

Acts I–V

1. Is imagination valued in the world today? Who helps to provide imaginative experiences? Of what value has imagination been in the world's history? Organize your thoughts by making lists or charts, and explore these ideas in a paper. Assume that you are writing for a magazine or newspaper supplement that publishes thoughtful essays.

Enrichment Activities

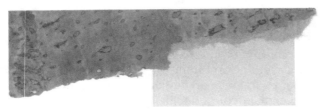

1. Costuming for the fairies in this play has challenged costume designers over the years. Design costumes that you think would be appropriate for these creatures, always remembering that the fairies are very active throughout the play.

2. Stage sets for this play have varied widely over the years. In some nineteenth-century productions, lavish designs included realistic flowers, trees, and moving scenery. In recent years, sets have become less elaborate but perhaps more imaginative. Design a set on paper or build a small model of a set you think would best suit the play.

3. Design a cover for a theatre program for a production of *A Midsummer Night's Dream*.

4. Study and perform for the class one of Titania's or Oberon's speeches or Bottom's speech in Act IV at the end of Scene 1.

5. With other class members, perform part of Act III, Scene 2, beginning with line 256 and ending with line 344. (In this scene, the four lovers are in the woods. Lysander and Demetrius are both in love with Helena and the two women exchange insults.)

6. Compose music for the song in Act II, Scene 2, and perform it for the class.

7. Should dramatic art deal with reality? Isn't life "real" enough without seeing it on the stage? Assume that you are a talk show host and prepare a list of questions about the relationship between art and reality and the function of the theatre in today's society. Conduct your show with class members supplying the discussion. If possible, have someone videotape the show.